CATHOLIC APOLOGETICS SERIES

BFSMedia Presents...

MyCatholicSource.com Article Reprint:

Setting The Record Straight About Luther

Important Things Catholics Should Know About The 'Reformer'

+ + +

BFSMedia & MyCatholicSource.com are divisions of B.F.S.

(C) 2016-2018, B.F.S. All Rights Reserved.

First Edition

+ + +

Notice: Use of this material is subject to our Terms of Use.

Dedication

This publication is gratefully dedicated to those defenders of the Catholic faith who have gone on before us. May God reward your good efforts on His behalf & continue to make them fruitful.

+ + +

Requiem aeternam dona eis Domine; et lux perpetua luceat eis. Requiescant in pace. Amen. (Eternal rest grant unto them, O Lord; and let perpetual light shine upon them. May they rest in peace. Amen.)

Terms of Use / Disclaimer

Material herein may be based on online versions of MyCatholicSource.com articles as they appeared at a point in time. Various items may differ from originals. Items herein are not comprehensive, may be limited in scope, may be categorized subjectively, and may overlap.

Capitalization, punctuation, wording, translations, titles, references, spelling, etc. of items herein may vary. Items may be partial / incomplete, in any order, not scholarly, subjective, etc. We may change punctuation, capitalization, spelling, referencing, wording, shorten items, combine items, etc. and we caution that items herein may be out of context, not in original context, incomplete, etc. We recommend reading applicable items in full context in appropriate Catholic materials.

Items indicated herein may be the opinions of their original authors. Inclusion of any item does not necessarily imply our endorsement or agreement.

This publication is 'Catholic-focused'. Some material herein may not be appropriate for children, sensitive persons, or for those not well catechized.

Consult appropriate, competent Church authorities for assistance in interpreting / applying all applicable items. Interpretation and application of items should not be contrary to the perennial, official teaching of the Roman Catholic Church. Do not take items out of context. Do not inflict harm on yourself or others, break laws, take unsuitable / incautious or inappropriate / drastic actions, or take figurative items literally. We are not responsible for any interpretation / misinterpretation, application / misapplication, use / misuse, etc. of any item.

Links provided herein may contain extraneous hyphens (which were added automatically during the publication process). Where applicable, it will be necessary to *exclude* extraneous hyphens to view the webpage(s). View all links at your own risk. Any visit to our website(s) may require agreement to our terms. For more terms information, visit http://www.mycatholicsource.com/mcs/terms_of_use.htm.

Any applicable items may vary and are subject to change at any time without notice.

We make no guarantee whatsoever regarding any item herein. All material is provided on an "as is" basis, without warranty of any kind. We are not liable for any loss or damage resulting from reliance on any information contained herein or for any loss or damage due to any error(s) or omission(s). We are not liable for any occurrence whatsoever which may result from any use of this material (including use of any links). All use of the material is at your own risk. By using any material (including links), you agree to hold us harmless for all consequences, damages, etc. - direct or indirect - which may occur in any way connected with any use of this material - regardless of their nature and without limit. By using any material herein, including links, you agree to all our terms. For more terms information, see terms link above.

Note to Readers

Please note that the material herein is based on a two-part article that was published in anticipation of the 500th anniversary of the 'Reformation' (a.k.a. Protestant Rebellion) in MyCatholicSource.com newsletters (9/16 & 10/16 editions). Note that this material may also be incorporated as a bonus in a larger work - our 'Catholics And Ecumenism' book (see Part 3 for more information).

As indicated below, the material that follows contains mature language and content. We do not recommend this publication for younger persons or sensitive persons. We also advise those not well-grounded in the Catholic faith to *NOT* read the following material in order to avoid being confused/led astray by the arch-heretic. Instead, try Part 2 for some refreshers.

We sincerely hope the material herein will prove useful.

May God grant you many blessings.

+ + +

"Almighty and everlasting God, whose will it is that all men should be saved and that none should perish, look upon the souls that are deceived by the guile of Satan, in order that the hearts of them that have gone astray may put aside all the perverseness of heresy, and, being truly repentant, may return to the unity of Thy truth. Through Christ our Lord. Amen." (Roman Missal)

+ + +

"A satanical hatred of the Pope and of all Roman Catholics is one of the characteristic features in the history and character of Luther." (Henry O'Connor, S.J.)

"[Luther was an] agitator, an overthrower, to whom no sophistry is too audacious, no artifice too bad, no lie too strong, no calumny too great, to justify his apostasy from the Church and from his own earlier principles." (Heinrich Denifle, O. P.)

"Luther assures us that Satan argued in favor of some of the principal doctrines of his new Creed." (Henry O'Connor, S.J.)

+ + +

Contents

Title Page..1
Dedication...2
Terms of Use / Disclaimer...3
Note to Readers 5
Part 1: Setting The Record Straight About Luther 8
Part 2: Some Refreshers 84
Part 3: In Closing...95

PART 1:
SETTING THE RECORD STRAIGHT ABOUT LUTHER

Important Things Catholics Should Know About The 'Reformer'

MyCatholicSource.com Article Reprint:

Setting The Record Straight About Luther

Important Things Catholics Should Know About The 'Reformer'

"Read Luther's work against 'the Mass and the Ordination of Priests' where he tells of his famous disputation with the 'Father of Lies' who accosted him at 'midnight' and spoke to him with a 'deep, powerful voice', causing 'the sweat to break forth' from his brow and his 'heart to tremble and beat.' In that celebrated conference of which he was an unexceptionable witness and about which he never entertained the slightest doubt, he says plainly and unmistakingly that 'the devil spoke against the Mass, and Mary and the Saints' and that, moreover, Satan gave him the most unqualified approval of his doctrine on 'justification by faith alone.' Who now, we ask in all sincerity, can be found, except those appallingly blind to truth, to accept such a man, approved by the enemy of souls, as a spiritual teacher and entrust to his guidance their eternal welfare?" (O'Hare)

As indicated above, material herein is based on a two-part article that was published in anticipation of the 500th anniversary of the 'Reformation' (a.k.a. Protestant Rebellion) in MyCatholicSource.com newsletters (9/16 & 10/16 editions). We sincerely hope you will find the following 'eye-opening' treatise concerning the Rebellion's catalyst/leader, Martin Luther, to be useful in combating erroneous opinions and all-too-common 'history re-writes'. *[Reminder: Do not inflict (or wish) harm on yourself or others, break laws, take unsuitable / incautious or inappropriate / drastic actions, or take figurative items literally. We are not responsible for any interpretation / misinterpretation, application / misapplication, use / misuse, etc. of any item. Use of this material is subject to our terms of use.]*

SETTING THE RECORD STRAIGHT ABOUT LUTHER

INTRODUCTION

As we approach the 500th anniversary of the so-called "Reformation" [the quincentennial anniversary occurred on 10/31/2017], it is unfortunately to be expected in our age that much misinformation concerning the events and the person of Martin Luther will be disseminated. For example, sadly (scandalously!), certain prelates in the Church have already hailed the arch-heretic as a "Gospel witness and teacher of the Faith." Therefore, it seems appropriate to counter such assertions with facts concerning Martin Luther, a prideful, vile, insidious, excommunicated, vow-breaking apostate priest, lying, hypocritical, hater of the Church, whose doctrines (which were approved by Satan) and whose warfare against the Church caused bloodshed, harmed families, led to a widespread loss of morality, and has surely resulted in the loss of countless souls.

[Note: Adjectives above may be based on writings of Catholic priests who have studied and written about Luther. See below for sources.]

ADVISORY: The following contains mature language and content. Luther's vileness/coarseness & false doctrines can also be *extremely* offensive. Regrettably, however, we nevertheless find it important to include such material here (occasionally in a masked fashion) in order paint a more accurate picture of Luther and his HIGHLY unsavory doctrines & behaviors. We apologize for any offense and advise younger persons and sensitive persons to skip this article and *NOT* read the material below. Also, those who are not well-grounded in the Catholic faith should NOT read the following in order to avoid being confused/led astray by the arch-heretic.

Please note that we have made various changes to applicable items below (e.g. punctuation, capitalization, spelling, paragraphing, wording changes, exclusion of special characters/footnotes, etc.). A brief outline of the article follows.

- - -

BRIEF OUTLINE

Introduction (above)

Some quick facts concerning Luther, which demonstrate that he was not sent by God

Some results of Luther's teachings

Some papal quotes regarding Martin Luther

More on Luther, his teachings / practices / behaviors, and their results

Conclusion

Note: Sources appear at end.

SOME QUICK FACTS CONCERNING LUTHER, WHICH DEMONSTRATE THAT HE WAS NOT SENT BY GOD

Note: Information regarding numeric references in brackets below may be found after the conclusion.

Luther...

- Rejected parts of scripture on his own authority

- *Blasphemously* charged Jesus with sin!!! (adultery) [Online Ref.: Trishreden, Weimer Edition, Vol. 2, Pg. 107]

- Had a hatred of the Church and the Mass ["A satanical hatred of the Pope and of all Roman Catholics is one of the characteristic features in the history and character of Luther." (1)]

- Encouraged others to sin ["Be a sinner and sin boldly, but believe and rejoice in Christ even more boldly... No sin will separate us from (Christ), even though we commit fornication and murder a thousand times a day." (Letter from Luther to Philip Melanchthon, August 1, 1521 A.D.)]

- Purposely mistranslated scripture to promote his doctrines

- Regularly mocked / ridiculed / insulted the Pope, bishops, priests, faithful, etc. and believed that "the true Antichrist, according to Paul, reigns in the Roman Court" (1)

- Wanted churches & convents destroyed

- Promoted bloodshed

- Permitted polygamy

- Sanctioned adultery & s*xual license

- Failed to condemn concubineage

- 'Raged war' against the Church

- Encouraged religious to break their vows

- Was an "agitator, an overthrower, to whom no sophistry is too audacious, no artifice too bad, no lie too strong, no calumny too great, to justify his apostasy from the Church and from his own earlier principles." (2)

- Mercilessly insulted his opponents ["His opponents were *sses, pigs, dolts, &c., and were assailed with still viler epithets." (4)]

- Use coarse invective ["Where he failed in argument he took refuge in invective, often of the coarsest kind." (4)]

- Made use of "vile illustrations to caricature the Pope, the monks, and the teachings of the Church." (4)

- PURPOSELY lied / deceived / misled and intentionally misrepresented / falsified / perverted / distorted / garbled Church teachings ["as Luther falsified Catholic teaching in general, so also did he falsify it in respect to the commandments, the counsels, and the vows." (2)]

- Promoted his dangerous conception of 'Christian liberty' [an "unbounded and unbridled licentiousness" (2)]

- Received satanic approval of his doctrines ["Luther assures us that Satan argued in favor of some of the principal doctrines of his new Creed. Now, it is beneath the dignity of God to allow His chosen legate to appeal to the testimony of Satan in support of his teaching." (1)]

- Used fraud to promote his teachings

- Engaged in calumny

- Was "a master in sophistry"

- Contradicted himself

- Taught false doctrines, endangering souls & resulting in a widespread moral decline (e.g. leading to corruption of manners, laxity in discipline, immodesty, unchastity, adultery, licentiousness, drunkenness, gluttony, cursing, lying, cheating, degradation of marriage, contempt for the sacraments, lessening of charity, shamelessness, ruination of family life, loss of fear of the Lord, etc.)

- Wanted the Ten Commandments to be removed "out of sight and heart". He called them "stupid" and said that, "If we allow them - the Commandments - any influence in our conscience, they become the cloak of all evil, heresies and blasphemies." (Comm. ad Galat., p. 310)

- Agitated the people, resulting in tumult, rebellion, riots, murder, reviling of/contempt for priests, hatred of the Church, disregard for authority, destruction of convents, altars & holy images

- Showed contempt for women

- Spoke in a vulgar manner [he made regular use of vulgar terms (e.g. f*rt, f*rt-*ss, excrement, urine, an*s, etc.)]

- Admitted he was "consumed by the fires of [his] unbridled flesh" and "consumed by the flesh and by lasciviousness" (De Wette, 2, 22)

- Was admittedly impure: "I burn with a thousand flames in my unsubdued flesh: I feel myself carried on with a rage towards women that approaches madness. I, who ought to be fervent in spirit, am only fervent in impurity." (Table Talk)

- Was "exceedingly wanton" ["Luther", as his associate Melanchthon writes, "was an exceedingly wanton man" (2)]

- Broke his vows and married an 'ex-nun' that he had previously lived with "in open and flagrant immorality", and he did so "out of contempt for the Papists" (2)

- Behaved badly personally (e.g. indulgent drinking & eating, insolence, laxity in prayers, blasphemy, outbursts of rage, mordacity, lust, etc.)

- Acted like a 'buffoon' ["He, Melanchthon, and his associates had often rebuked him on account of his buffoonery." (2)]

- Thought he was superior and falsely imagined he was infallible

- Ultimately entertained doubts/regrets after seeing the terrible results of his teaching, yet did not recant

Some further thoughts...

- Luther does NOT meet the criteria of a holy man, his doctrine is NOT holy, and the results of his doctrine are NOT holy. People did NOT become more devout, pious, or holy under his teachings - quite the opposite.

- "A man who pretends to be a Reformer is sent either by God or by Satan. Now, every single sign of a Divine mission is utterly wanting, both in Luther's teaching, and in the results of his teaching." (1)

- "Every reasonable person will agree with me, that Luther can only have been a Reformer chosen by Almighty God, if his teaching caused an increase of virtue and a decrease of vice. If, however, it can be plainly shown, that in consequence of his teaching there was, on the contrary, an increase of vice and a decrease of virtue, we must come to the conclusion, that Luther had not the sanction of God for the work which he undertook." (1)

SOME RESULTS OF LUTHER'S TEACHINGS

The following quotation provides a summary of some results of Luther's teachings...

> "Luther was the author of the...texts for the violation of the vows, the wiving of priests and monks. He put the words on the prohibition of the vow of chastity into the large catechism. He set up the principle that God imposed an impossible thing upon us, that the (s*xual) instinct of nature cannot be resisted, that it must be satisfied. He depicted himself as burning with carnal concupiscence, although some years before he had condemned it and discovered its genesis in the lack of communion with God; he admitted that his own fervor of spirit was decreasing and that he was neglecting prayer.
>
> As his teachings were depopulating the monasteries, so he himself furnished the incentive to the abduction of the consecrated virgins, the perpetrator being called by him a 'blessed robber,' and compared with Christ, who robbed the prince of the world of what was his. *[From footnote: The rape and*

abduction of the consecrated nuns was carried out by the burgher Koppe in the night of Holy Saturday, 1523. Luther carried his blasphemy so far, that he wrote to the abductor: 'Like Christ you have also led these poor souls out of the prison of human tyranny at just the appropriate time of Easter, when Christ led captive the captivity of His own.'] He took one of the abducted nuns, put up for sale, as a witness of his gospel, as his concubine, and called her his wife.

He severed the bonds of marriage and destroyed its indissolubility by his theory, which in practice found expression in the wh*redoms and adulteries so bitterly complained of. He did not forbid the taking of several wives and declared that polygamy was not strictly opposed to the word of God.

As a panacea for all sin, he prescribed only trust in Christ's forgiveness, without requiring love. He condemned the contrition, confession, and penance of the Catholic Church, reviled the Pope as Antichrist, rejected the priesthood, the Mass, the religious state and every good work. It was his teaching that good works, even at their best, are sins, and even that a just man sins in all good works. As he had imposed sin upon Christ, so also did he put the fulfillment of our prayers upon Him. And with all of that, he extols himself as a saint, and presumes, if he did not do so, he would be blaspheming Christ.

If ever a doctrine had to lead to the acme of wickedness, it was such a one as this. It is not to be wondered at, that more than elsewhere, this became manifest to all eyes at Wittenberg, Luther's residence. As early as 1524, a former Wittenberg student, the Rottenburg German grammarian, Valentine Ickelsamer, wrote to Luther: 'What Rome had to hear for a long time, we say of you: 'The nearer to Wittenberg, the worse the Christians."' Luther's teaching brought the current of decline down to a state which he himself recognized and openly proclaimed to be far worse than that under the Papacy. Of this he could make no concealment, for the facts spoke too loudly, no matter what ridiculous pretensions he might allege in explanation or extenuation of them. Not once merely, but often he says that his Lutherans were seven times worse than before. 'There was indeed one devil driven out of us, but now seven of them more wicked have gone into us.' Even in 1523, he had to acknowledge that he and his followers were become worse than they had been formerly. This he later repeats. 'The world by this teaching becomes only the worse, the longer it exists; that is the work and business of the malign devil. As one sees, the people are more avaricious, less merciful, more immodest, bolder and worse than before under the Papacy.' He perceived that 'wickedness and wanton license are increasing with excessive swiftness,' and this indeed, 'in all states,' so that 'the people are all becoming devils,' but he meant knavish, 'only to spite our teaching!' 'Avarice, usury, immodesty, gluttony, cursing, lying, cheating are abroad in all their might,' yes, more than of old under the Papacy; such disordered conduct on the part of almost everybody, causes gossip about the gospel and the preachers, it being said: 'if this teaching were right, the people would be more devout.' 'Therefore it is that every one now complains that the gospel causes much unrest, bickering and disordered conduct, and, since it has come up, everything is worse than ever before,' etc.

Despite his assurance that his teaching was the genuine gospel, he still had to acknowledge that 'the people opposed it so shamefully that the more it is preached, the worse they become and the weaker our faith is.' He and his followers with their preaching, he says, cannot do so much as make a single home pious; on the contrary, 'if one had now to baptize the adults and the old, I think it probable that not a tenth of them would let themselves be baptized.'

Apart from Erasmus and Pirkheimer, others no less impartial than Luther also pronounced the same judgment. The blustering apostate Franciscan, Henry Von Kettenbach, in 1525, preached: 'Many people now act as if all sins and wickedness were permitted, as if there were no hell, no devil, no God, and they are more evil than they have ever been, and still wish to be good Evangelicals.' Another fallen Franciscan, Eberlin Von Gunzburg wrote similarly that the Evangelicals, in their riotous living, since they became free from the Pope, were become 'doubly worse than the Papists, yes, worse than Tyre, Sidon, and Sodom.' If, according to the admission of Luther himself and his followers the moral condition of Lutheranism was far worse than that under the Papacy, the blacker the epoch before Luther is painted, the blacker must Lutherdom appear.

The condition was indeed such that, as early as 1527, Luther expressed a doubt whether he would have begun, had he foreseen all the great scandals and disorders. 'Yes, who would have wanted to begin preaching,' said he eleven years later, 'had we known beforehand that so much misfortune, factiousness, scandal, calumny, ingratitude and wickedness were to follow. But now that we are in it, we have to pay for it.'" (2)

SOME PAPAL QUOTES REGARDING MARTIN LUTHER

The following are some papal quotes regarding Martin Luther...

- "Rise, Peter, and fulfill this pastoral office divinely entrusted to you as mentioned above. Give heed to the cause of the holy Roman Church, mother of all churches and teacher of the faith, whom you by the order of God, have consecrated by your blood. Against the Roman Church, you warned, lying teachers are rising, introducing ruinous sects, and drawing upon themselves speedy doom. Their tongues are fire, a restless evil, full of deadly poison. They have bitter zeal, contention in their hearts, and boast and lie against the truth." (3)

- "Rebuking them, in violation of your teaching, instead of imploring them, he is not ashamed to assail them, to tear at them, and when he despairs of his cause, to stoop to insults. He is like the heretics 'whose last defense,' as Jerome says, 'is to start spewing out a serpent's venom with their tongue when they see that their causes are about to be condemned, and spring to insults when they see they are vanquished.'" (3)

- "Some, putting aside her true interpretation of Sacred Scripture, are blinded in mind by the father of lies. Wise in their own eyes, according to the ancient practice of heretics, they interpret these same Scriptures otherwise than the Holy Spirit demands, inspired only by their own sense of ambition, and for the sake of popular acclaim, as the Apostle declares. In fact, they twist and adulterate the Scriptures. As a result, according to Jerome, 'It is no longer the Gospel of Christ, but a man's, or what is worse, the devil's.'" (3)

- "Their talkativeness, unsupported by the authority of the Scriptures, as Jerome says, would not win credence unless they appeared to support their perverse doctrine even with divine testimonies however badly interpreted. From their sight fear of God has now passed." (3)

- "In virtue of our pastoral office committed to us by the divine favor we can under no circumstances tolerate or overlook any longer the pernicious poison of the above errors without disgrace to the Christian religion and injury to orthodox faith." (3)

- "Moreover, because the preceding errors and many others are contained in the books or writings of Martin Luther, we likewise condemn, reprobate, and reject completely the books and all the writings and sermons of the said Martin, whether in Latin or any other language, containing the said errors or any one of them; and we wish them to be regarded as utterly condemned, reprobated, and rejected." (3)

- "As far as Martin himself is concerned, O good God, what have we overlooked or not done? What fatherly charity have we omitted that we might call him back from such errors? For after we had cited him, wishing to deal more kindly with him, we urged him through various conferences with our legate and through our personal letters to abandon these errors. We have even offered him safe conduct and the money necessary for the journey urging him to come without fear or any misgivings, which perfect charity should cast out, and to talk not secretly but openly and face to face after the example of our Savior and the Apostle Paul. If he had done this, we are certain he would have changed in heart, and he would have recognized his errors. He would not have found all these errors in the Roman Curia which he attacks so viciously, ascribing to it more than he should because of the empty rumors of wicked men. We would have shown him clearer than the light of day that the Roman pontiffs, our predecessors, whom he injuriously attacks beyond all decency, never erred in their canons or constitutions which he tries to assail. For, according to the prophet, neither is healing oil nor the doctor lacking in Galaad. But he always refused to listen and, despising the previous citation and each and every one of the above overtures, disdained to come. To the present day he has been contumacious. With a hardened spirit he has continued under censure over a year." (3)

- "Hence it befits the Pontiff, lest the vessel of Peter appear to sail without pilot or oarsman, to take severe measures against such men and their followers, and by multiplying punitive measures and by other suitable remedies to see to it that these same overbearing men, devoted as they are to purposes of evil, along with their adherents, should not deceive the multitude of the simple by their lies and their deceitful devices, nor drag them along to share their own error and ruination, contaminating them with what amounts to a contagious disease." (5)

- "Nevertheless Martin himself - and it gives us grievous sorrow and perplexity to say this - the slave of a depraved mind, has scorned to revoke his errors within the prescribed interval and to send us word of such revocation, or to come to us himself; nay, like a stone of stumbling, he has feared not to write and preach worse things than before against us and this Holy See and the Catholic faith, and to lead others on to do the same." (5)

- "He [Luther] has now been declared a heretic; and so also others, whatever their authority and rank, who have cared nought of their own salvation but publicly and in all men's eyes become followers of Martin's pernicious and heretical sect, and given him openly and publicly their help, counsel and favors, encouraging him in their midst in his disobedience and obstinacy, or hindering the publication of our said missive: such men have incurred the punishments set out in that missive, and are to be treated rightfully as heretics and avoided by all faithful Christians, as the Apostle says (Titus iii. 10-11)." (5)

MORE ON LUTHER, HIS TEACHINGS / PRACTICES / BEHAVIORS, AND THEIR RESULTS

LUTHER RECEIVED APPROVAL OF HIS TEACHING FROM SATAN

"Now, I do not, say that Luther here for the first time learnt the doctrine of justification by faith alone, or that he was taught for the first time on this occasion to do away with Mass, with Mary and the Saints. It is quite possible that some, or all of these doctrines, were preached by Luther before this celebrated disputation. But this I do say, and I say it most distinctly and most emphatically: Luther received the full and unqualified approval of the Devil for these new doctrines. It was the Devil who spoke in favor of the doctrine of justification by faith alone, and against Mass, Mary, and the Saints...Luther himself believed that it was the Devil, and the Great Reformer of Germany continued preaching, although he firmly believed that the Devil had spoken in favor of the principal articles of his new Creed... Luther's book against Private Mass may be divided into two parts;

in the first, Luther gives the Devil's reasons; in the second he gives his own. This extraordinary arrangement of a work containing about one hundred pages, shows us how fully Luther agrees with the Devil's teaching concerning Mass." (1)

"Having rejected the authority of the Pope, he admits the authority of Satan; for he informs us in plain, unmistakeable words, that the Devil argued in favor of his doctrine of justification by faith alone, and against Mass, Mary, and the Saints." (1)

"Read Luther's work against 'the Mass and the Ordination of Priests' where he tells of his famous disputation with the 'Father of Lies' who accosted him at 'midnight' and spoke to him with a 'deep, powerful voice', causing 'the sweat to break forth' from his brow and his 'heart to tremble and beat.' In that celebrated conference of which he was an unexceptionable witness and about which he never entertained the slightest doubt, he says plainly and unmistakingly that 'the devil spoke against the Mass, and Mary and the Saints' and that, moreover, Satan gave him the most unqualified approval of his doctrine on 'justification by faith alone.' Who now, we ask in all sincerity, can be found, except those appallingly blind to truth, to accept such a man, approved by the enemy of souls, as a spiritual teacher and entrust to his guidance their eternal welfare?" (O'Hare)

Some Reminders:

"[T]he chief aim of the evil one is to deprive us of our heavenly inheritance." (Catechism of the Council of Trent)

"Be sober and vigilant. Your opponent the devil is prowling around like a roaring lion looking for (someone) to devour." (St. Peter, 1 Pt. 5:8)

"[The devil] was a murderer from the beginning and does not stand in truth, because there is no truth in him. When he tells a lie, he speaks in character, because he is a liar and the father of lies." (Our Lord Jesus Christ, Jn. 8:44)

LUTHER'S WORK IS SATANICAL

"Only one year before his death, Luther published a famous work against the Pope. This work is so satanical in its title ['Against the Popery of Rome, instituted by the Devil'], so satanical in its beginning, so satanical in its almost every page, so super-satanical in its conclusion, that it could have only been written by a man with a thoroughly satanical spirit. It is marvelous how anyone should have been able to fill one hundred and fifty-seven printed pages with such a number of satanical expressions that must have been borrowed from the very depths of Hell." (1)

LUTHER ENGAGED IN VULGAR 'COMBATS' WITH THE DEVIL, RECEIVED HIS 'INSPIRATION' WHILE ON THE TOILET, AND COULD NOT LOOK UPON A CRUCIFIX

"The founder and primus inter pares ('first among equals') of this priesthood, Martin Luther, was originally a servant of the Church, though not out of a sense of fidelity or spiritual calling. He became a monk to escape and affront his abusive parents - both of whom beat him severely. Luther's father was not a Catholic, but an occultist who believed in darker Germanic witches, hobgoblins, and demons. These would also haunt the imagination of Martin Luther who had visions, which he believed to be actual physical occurrences, of the devil hurling 'sh*t' at him and his hurling it back. Indeed, in one of his many an*l combats with the devil - in which Luther would challenge the devil to 'lick' his posterior - Luther thought the best tactic might be to 'throw him into my an*s, where he belongs.' ... Luther's mind and manner, needless to say, were not those of a noble, polished Renaissance courtier, but those of a rough, gnarled, hamfisted working-class northern German. Being, in the words of the historian William Manchester, 'the most an*l of theologians,' it is not surprising that, like the American President Lyndon Baines Johnson, Luther conducted his business while defecating. His 'thunderbolt' idea that faith alone was sufficient for salvation came, in his own words, as 'knowledge the Holy Spirit (!!!) gave me on the privy in the tower.'... [Also,] Luther was prone to panic attacks. He could not look upon a crucifix. He tried to avoid performing a Mass or being in the presence of the Blessed Sacrament. His life was one continual terror of damnation." (Crocker, "Triumph: The Power and the Glory of the Catholic Church")

LUTHER ENCOURAGES SIN

"Be a sinner and sin boldly, but believe and rejoice in Christ even more boldly... No sin will separate us from [Christ], even though we commit fornication and murder a thousand times a day." (Letter from Luther to Philip Melanchthon, August 1, 1521 A.D.)

LUTHER WRONGLY THINKS PEOPLE 'HAVE TO SIN' AND THAT THE 'ENTIRE DECALOGUE' (10 COMMANDMENTS) CAN BE DISMISSED

"Let us hear the 'Reformer': 'As often as the devil vexes you with those thoughts, seek immediately the company of people, or drink harder, joke, make fun or get jolly. At times one has to drink more copiously, jest, play the fool, and commit some sin or another out of hatred and contempt of the devil, so that we leave him no room to create a conscience in us on the least things, otherwise we are beaten, if we wish too anxiously to make provision lest we sin. Therefore if the devil says: 'drink not,' answer him: 'precisely because you forbid it, will I particularly drink, yes, and all the more copiously.' Thus must one always do the opposite of what the devil forbids.' To arouse the troubled one's courage, Luther sets himself up as an example: 'What else do you think were the reason why I drink so much harder, prate the more loosely, gormandize the more frequently, if not to mock and vex the devil who set about mocking and vexing me? Oh, if only I could point out something particular about sin, merely to mock the devil, so that he might be aware that I recognize no sin and am not conscious of any! The entire decalogue is wholly to be dismissed from sight and mind by us, whom the devil so threatens and vexes.'" (2)

LUTHER CALLS FOR BLOODSHED AGAINST CATHOLICS

"If we punish thieves with the gallows, robbers with the sword, heretics with fire, why do we not still more attack with every kind of weapon these teachers of perdition, these Cardinals, these Popes, and that whole abomination of the Romish Sodom, which, without ceasing, corrupts the Church of God, and why do we not wash our hands in their blood?" (Luther) (1)

"Whereas I have said...that Popery and the clerical body will not be upset by the hand of man, nor by rebellion, but that its wickedness is so abominable that no punishment is sufficient for it, except only the anger of God, without any (human) intervention; I have never yet been induced to keep those back who threaten with the fist and with flails..." (Luther) (1)

LUTHER CALLS FOR KILLING OF THOSE IN REBELLION

"Therefore, whoever can, ought to strike in here, to strangle and stab, secretly or openly, and he ought to remember that there is nothing more poisonous, disastrous, diabolical than a man in rebellion..." (Luther) (1)

LUTHER SHOWS CONTEMPT FOR WOMEN

"God's work and word lie before our eyes; women must be used either for marriage or for wh*rishness." (Luther) (2)

"Contempt for woman began then, when Luther coarsely and unfeelingly degraded her to the level of a breeding cow: 'If women breed themselves sick and eventually to death, that does no harm; let them breed themselves to death, that is what they are for. It is better to live a short time in health than a long time in sickness." (2)

LUTHER WANTS WOMEN REMOVED FROM THE RELIGIOUS STATE EVEN AT THE COST OF ONE'S LIFE

"Behold now a part of the misery. The greater part of our lasses are in monasteries, they are fresh and healthy, created by God to be wives and to bear children, are not able, either, willingly to put up with their state; for chastity is a grace above nature, if it were equally pure... Now if you had a daughter or a friend, gone into such a state, you ought, if you were honest and devout, to assist her out of it, even if you had to apply for the purpose all your goods, your body and life." (Luther) (2)

LUTHER CALLS FOR ACTIVE PERSECUTION OF THE JEWS

Luther instructs that Jews' "houses are likewise to he broken down and destroyed", that "Jews are to be entirely denied legal protection when using the roads in the country", and that "all their cash and their treasures of silver and gold are to be taken away from them..." He also instructs: "Force them to work, and treat them with every kind of severity..." (1)

LUTHER FALSELY CONSIDERS MONASTIC VOWS AS NULL AND VOID

"In his writing on the monastic vows, Luther wishes to prove that they are null and void and contradict the teaching of Christ and His Gospel. In his judgment they are heathenish, Jewish, blasphemous, founded on lies, erroneous, devilish, hypocritical; members of religious orders can therefore, with a good conscience, abandon their monasteries and marry." (2)

LUTHER'S COMMENTS ARE INSULTING/OFFENSIVE

"Luther says: 'The Pope's Christ is the mother of the Devil.' That is to say, the Christ, in whom the Pope and the Catholics believe, is the mother of the Devil. Again: 'The Pope, the Cardinals, and the whole Romish Court and, mob, are nothing else but a stable full of big, coarse, stupid, disgraceful donkeys.' There is no mistaking the meaning of the following passage: 'You are indeed a coarse donkey, and you remain a donkey, you donkey of a Pope.'" (1)

Luther says: "The Pope, the Cardinals ought to be taken and (as they are blasphemers) their tongue ought to be torn out through the back of their neck and nailed to the gallows..." (1)

One author (a priest) states the following regarding Luther's works: "I have come across several such utterly vulgar, coarse, and disreputable expressions in this work of Luther, that I would not venture to give them, even in the original German. I can only say in conclusion, that I believe this is one of the most monstrous books that has ever been written. In satanical expressions it will never be surpassed, except, perhaps, by Antichrist himself. If this book were accurately translated into English, extensively published, and carefully read by every Protestant Englishman, the whole nation would turn away with horror and disgust from the monster, who was capable of writing such a scandalous work." (1)

Note: Above is only a tiny sample. Insulting/offensive quotes from Luther may be multiplied many times over.

LUTHER INTENTIONALLY MISTRANSLATES SCRIPTURE ('RECKLESS TAMPERING WITH SCRIPTURE') ON HIS OWN AUTHORITY TO SUPPORT HIS DOCTRINES

"And in order to return to the point. If your Papist makes much unnecessary fuss about the word (Sola, alone), say straight out to him, Doctor Martinus Luther will have it so, and says, Papists and donkeys are one and the same thing. Thus I will have it, thus I order it, my will is reason enough (trans.). For we will not be the scholars or the disciples of the Papists, but their masters and judges. We must once in a way act a little haughtily and noisily with these jack-*sses." (Luther) (1)

"This is my answer to your first question; and as to their unnecessary noise about the word Sola, I beg of you not to give those donkeys any other or further answer, but simply this much: D. Luther will have it so, and says he is a Doctor above all Doctors in the whole of Popery." (Luther) (1)

"I knew very well that here, Rom. III., the word (Sola) is not in the Latin and Greek text, and it was not necessary for the Papists to teach me that. It is true, these four, letters, S O L A, are not in it, which letters the jack-*sses look at as a cow looks at a new gate..." (Luther) (1)

LUTHER FALSELY IMAGINES THAT HE IS INFALLIBLE

"Whoever teaches differently from what I have taught herein, or condemns me for it, he condemns God, and must be a child of Hell." (Luther) (1)

"I herewith let you know that in future, I will no longer do you the honor of allowing you, or even an Angel from Heaven, to judge my doctrine... There has been enough of this stupid humility now for the third time at Worms, and, nevertheless, it was of no use; but I will make myself heard, and, as St. Peter teaches, I will prove the motives and reasons for my teaching before the whole world, and I will not allow it to be judged by anybody, not even by any of the Angels. For, since I am certain of it, I intend, by means of it, to be your judge and also (as St. Paul says), that of the Angels; so that whoever does not accept my teaching, cannot be saved. For it is God's and not mine. Therefore, my judgment is at the same time God's and not mine." (Luther) (1)

LUTHER INSULTS BOTH PRELATES AND THE FAITHFUL

"All those that step in to defend the authority of the Bishops and are subject to them with willing obedience are the real servants of the Devil, and fight against the order and law of God." (Luther) (1)

"Nobody can be a Papist, without being at least a murderer, a robber, a persecutor... It is clear enough that they (the Papists) are the Christians of the Devil." (Luther) (1)

"Luther says that Bishops under the Pope are 'Wolves, tyrants, murderers of souls, and the Apostles of Antichrist to corrupt the world. And, not to mince matters, everybody ought to know that the Bishops who now rule over many towns are not Christian Bishops according to Divine order, but according to devilish order and human wickedness. It is also certain that they are the messengers and vicars of the Devil.'" (1)

"From the end of 1518, he [Luther] had regarded the Pope as Antichrist." (2)

"When he [Luther] concludes 'Thus let the *ss-pope and the Pope-*ss and his juristic *sses be welcomed this time,' the 'Reformer' brands himself, as so frequently he does, a low blackguard." (2)

LUTHER CALLS FOR HATRED OF THE POPE

"Clement VII. died in 1534, and was succeeded by Paul III., who was anxious to convene a council, that the Protestants might attend. But they rejected all overtures. The League of Smalkald was renewed (1535) for ten years. In 1534 Luther completed his translation of the whole Bible, and in 1537 issued the Articles of Smalkald, which were accepted by the League, and which embodied a spirit of deep hostility to the Catholic Church. 'May God fill you with hatred of the Pope!' was his parting benediction to the League, and thenceforth the League refused to attend any council of the Church." (4)

LUTHER WAS FULL OF HATRED

"The 'Reformer' and his followers were the very ones who conducted themselves as though the Divine Redeemer had positively commanded revenge and forbidden the love of one's enemy. To be convinced of this, one needs but read any book whatever by Luther, that hatred-filled and most biting of men." (2)

CONTRARY TO CHRIST'S TEACHING, LUTHER ALLOWS MULTIPLE WIVES AND PROMOTES S*XUAL LICENSE

Scandalously (and quite contrary to Christ's teachings), Luther says: "Nevertheless, in certain cases there is room for dispensation. If a person were a prisoner among foreign nations, and were to take another wife, for the welfare and health of his body, or if a person had a wife suffering from leprosy, we do not know on what ground it would be justifiable to condemn such a man, were he, in these cases, to marry another woman, with the advice of his pastor, having no intention to introduce a new law, but (only) seeking a remedy for his necessity.'" (1)

"Finally, if your Highness has altogether made up your mind to marry another wife, we declare under an oath that it ought to be done secretly... No contradictions or scandals of any importance will be the consequence of this (of keeping the marriage secret), for it is nothing unusual for princes to have concubines; and although the reason could not be understood by ordinary people, nevertheless, more prudent persons would understand it, and this modest way of living (!!!) would please more than adultery...nor are the sayings of others to be cared for, if our conscience is in order. Thus and thus far only do we approve of it." (Luther) (1) *[Note here how the arch-heretic counsels secrecy for the scandalous deeds, fails to condemn concubineage, scandalously says bigamy is a 'modest way of living', and claims one's conscience can be in order while intending to engage in bigamy - clearly this is NOT God's teaching.]*

"Kostlin, Luther's most prominent German champion, confesses that 'this double marriage' [bigamy] is the 'greatest blot in the history of the Reformation and in the life of Luther.' We may add that the blot is so great, as to blot out every possibility of our ever looking upon Luther as a Reformer sanctioned and commissioned by Almighty God. For marriage is one of the most important and most essential elements both of the social and of the religious order. And God would not allow a Reformer really chosen by Himself to trample under foot the law concerning the unity of marriage, which was promulgated by Christ, the first-born Reformer of the World." (1)

"He [Luther] writes in such a strain that, after receiving an 'exemption' in 'confession,' it scarcely any longer appears to be adultery for a married man, in 'necessity,' to keep a concubine. As Luther terms it, the concubine then becomes a 'conjugal concubine,' with whom the married man 'may sleep as with his wife, and whom he need not put away.'" (2)

"As early as 1520, he had set up the proposition: 'I abhor divorce so greatly that I prefer bigamy to it, but whether it be allowed, I do not venture to decide.' After setting up the principle, however, that there is no resisting the s*xual instinct, he did not hit upon the decision, when he found that polygamy was not against the Scriptures; he himself, he said, could not forbid it, although on account of the scandal, and for the sake of honor, he was unwilling to counsel it to anyone. 'The husband himself must be sure and certain in his own conscience, by the word of God, that this is allowed him.' He may therefore look up such as 'by God's word make him positive.' The husband naturally found them at once! In 1526, Luther repeats that the husband 'must have a divine word for himself, making him certain, just as the old fathers (of the Old Testament) had it.' In 1527, likewise, he finds that it is not forbidden that a man is allowed to have more than one wife; 'I could not now forbid it, but I would not wish to counsel it.'" (2)

Note that "... Luther was the first to grant a dispensation in respect to polygamy, while no medieval theologian maintained it was allowed in the New Testament." (2)

LUTHER HOLDS ERRONEOUS VIEWS ON HOLY MATRIMONY AND DEBASES THE SACRAMENT OF MARRIAGE

"The year following he wrote: 'Spite of the praise of married life, I do not wish to have given to nature that there is no sin there, but I say: flesh and blood are there, corrupted by Adam, conceived and born in sin (Ps. 50/51:7), and that no conjugal debt takes place without sins; but God spares them of His grace, because the marital order is His work and, in the midst of and throughout sin, preserves all the good which He therein implanted and blessed.' The next year he repeats that God blessed marriage, although he knew that 'nature, corrupted, full of evil passion, cannot consummate such a blessing without sin.' 'God covers up the sin without which the married cannot be,' he writes later. Now who reduces marriage to a merely tolerated, yes, to a sinful state? The Church? No. The monk Luther has quite sufficiently enlightened us [i.e. misled us] on the matter. The Church does not teach 'that no conjugal debt takes place without sin.' Rather is that taught by the apostate monk Luther, who at the same time, by his low conception of it, degrades marriage to such a degree that, according to him, there were no difference between the married state and wh*redom, were God not willing to close His eyes to it. He stated this expressly...and he repeats it frequently, and in a manner even more drastic. The conjugal act, according to him, is materially the same as the act of wh*rishness; it is only 'per indulgentiam' that no adultery, no pollution occurs. 'Because the commerce is of God's ordaining, He does not impute what is odious and impure in it.' The mutual commerce is only a concession 'per indulgentiam divinam,' says Luther, yet there is sin in the flesh on both sides. Who, then, makes the conjugal act materially the same as the act of wh*rishness? The Church? Scholasticism? Just the contrary. Scholasticism never departed from the principle uttered by St. Augustine: 'The conjugal act for the sake of begetting children or of rendering the marriage debt entails no fault or sin.' For God Himself instituted marriage for the propagation of the human race, and after the fall He also gave the commandment of the procreation of children, which commandment, however, cannot be kept without the conjugal act. From this alone it follows that if everything is done in the proper manner and in the order instituted by God, sin is excluded." (2)

"Luther did indeed put marriage in a new light, but only in this that he stripped it of honor." (2)

"Consistently Luther had to divest matrimony of its sacramental character and to degrade it to the level of 'an external bodily thing, like any other secular affair,' so that a Christian can marry a heathen, a Jew, or a Turk. The results of such teachings are known." (2)

"As a matter of fact, as early as 1520, Luther advised the woman who could get no children by her husband but could not keep continent, to seek a divorce from him, so as to be free to marry another. If the husband was unwilling, she should get his consent - for after all he was no longer her wedded spouse [according to Luther] - to her cohabiting (misceatur) with another or with his brother, in secret marriage, and the child should be ascribed to the first husband. If he is unwilling to give such consent: 'Rather than permit her to burn (with lust) or to commit adultery, I would advise her to marry another and to flee to some unknown place. What else can be advised to one who continually suffers from the danger of carnal lust?' To fly into a strange country, and there, should he be unable to keep continent, to marry, is likewise Luther's advice to an adulterer, if he is not killed. If a wife is unwilling to do her marriage duty, let the husband think 'that his wife has been abducted from him by robbers, and he must set about getting another.' To marry again is generally permitted to the one who, after the separation of a couple, wishes to be reconciled to the other, the other not consenting to the reconciliation. The ground of another marriage on the part of the one willing to be reconciled, according to Luther, is, as always, the same: if such a one cannot keep continent, the impossibility, to which God will force no one.'" (2)

"'How, if one party (husband or wife) was unwilling to be reconciled with the other (after they had separated), and simply desired to remain apart, and the other could not keep continent and had to have a consort, what should the latter do? Is there any change possible? Yes, without doubt. For, since it is not commanded that they live chastely, and one has not the grace either, and the other is unwilling to come and thus deprives the consort of the body which the consort cannot do without, God will not compel the impossible for the sake of another's misdeed; the (injured) party, not being to blame that they do not come together, must then act as if the other were dead. But the unwilling party is to remain without marriage, as St. Paul here says.' But I Cor. 7, 10 and 11, run quite otherwise." (2)

"Luther's confession counsel is absolutely his own creation, a sequel to his unblushing and wanton undertaking to rob marriage of its sacramental character. It was accordingly given out that now and then a second wife was even for Christians a wholesome medicine, a sacred remedy against wh*rishness.'" (2) [Refresher: "Christ Himself taught and required this indissolubility (of marriage), whereas Protestantism teaches the dissolubility of marriage, and permits the divorced to marry again accordingly. More than from anything else, from the sacramental character of marriage and from its likeness to the covenant between Christ and His Church, there follows its monogamic character, i.e., the complete exclusion of polygamy; for Christ cleaves only to the one Church and bestows His whole love upon her. In like manner man and wife become one flesh and are one in love like Christ and His Church." (2)]

"What Luther knavishly charged against Catholics was itself verified in Lutherdom: it seemed almost to belong to perfection to go from the marriage-bed to the wh*re house. Luther's degradation of marriage to an external, bodily thing, like any other secular affair, was everywhere put into practice. Like an artisan not seldom abandoning his present occupation and turning to another, or even to two or three together, for the sake of the advantage or on account of the cares of his maintenance, so in Lutheranism husbands left their wives or wives their husbands to try another; nay, more, 'and a shame it is to say it, they have not only given two wives to one man, but, what the world has never heard and heathens never permitted, they have given two men to one woman; they have allowed the man, when the wife was refractory, to go to the maid-servant, and where the man was impotent, the wife might go to another,' as the Dominican, J. Mensing, writes. Things of this kind and even worse occurred likewise among the Protestant 'clergy' and preachers. And Luther's principles were to blame. The first preachers were mostly 'married' priests and religious, who, with Luther, held the oath they had once sworn to God to be nothing. Were they to have more regard for the oath they swore to their wives? Why should one be astonished if, in the end, such a 'clergyman' had three living 'wives,' like ['Pastor'] Michael Kramer? Why should one marvel that Luther, in his decision of August 18, 1525, approved Kramer's second divorce and his 'marriage' to another woman, just as he had approved the first divorce and his 'marriage' to his second wife? Principles of that kind led the one-time Lutheran preacher, Sebastian Flasch, a native of Mansfield, to complain in 1576: 'Although even the preachers are 'married,' they are nevertheless so little contented with their better halves that, under Luther's guidance, to satisfy their insatiable desire, they often misuse their maid-servants, and, what is shameful, they do not blush to do violence to the wives of others, and to arrange among themselves for an exchange of wives (commutationem uxorum). I should not make bold openly to assert and write this about them if, during my long association with them, I had not had frequent and certain experience of this and much else.'" (2)

"From this [false teaching] it necessarily follows that, when a woman releases her husband, he is also set free with God; both are lawfully divorced! Rightly therefore does the famous Pistorius [once a Protestant, Pistorius later became the 'feared, invincible opponent of the Protestant pastors and theologians after his return to the Church.'] say: 'All external sins therefore depend solely on the consent of that person against whom the act is committed. If this person is satisfied, it is no sin before God or the world to take many wives, to divorce wives from one's self, to violate an oath, to murder, wh*re, or steal!' The above teaching of Luther's is also at the same time the best commentary on his proposition, that marriage is an external thing like any secular affair. The readers now also understand that, by such principles, all fear of God was violently torn from the hearts of the married and consequently the door to all vices was opened to them." (2)

"What indeed could more weaken the marriage bond than such a hair-raising doctrine? If the fear of God has disappeared from the hearts of the married, the one will not even await the other's consent to the dissolution of the marriage tie. Whether the latter be obstinate or not, the former will go the ways forecast by lust. That is quite logical, however, if marriage is looked upon as an affair like any other. In 1522, Luther knows no higher point of comparison for it than that of eating, drinking, sleeping, walking, riding, buying, talking, and trafficking. But something else follows from this. If the chief principle for the permissibility of a marriage was, that one could marry the person with whom he could eat, drink, sleep, walk, etc., then the marriage impediments, recognized up to that time, had to fall as the work of fools, and one would wonder greatly if Luther had not allowed the marriage bond between brother and sister. But to this proposition he likewise agreed. In 1528, all the marriage impediments juris ecclesiastici were declared by him to be dead, i.e., set aside; also even such as are juris naturalis, or nearly akin to it, consanguinitas, affinitas, and publicae honestatis." (2)

"Moreover, the lawfulness of marriage between brother and sister according to Luther is a consequence of his principles, and only the imperial law would have been able to determine him for its unlawfulness. From his 'tod' ['dead, i.e., set aside'] on proposition a, it would also have been possible to prove that, according to him, even marriage between father and daughter, mother and son was lawful." (2)

"It has been kept unaware [from some people] of how unjust and fallacious Luther's warfare was against the marriage laws of the Church and against marriage as a sacrament, and how disintegrating his principles were in their effect upon marriage and the family life of his time and the time immediately following." (2)

LUTHER WAS A LIAR WHO MADE USE OF FABRICATIONS, SOPHISMS, FALSIFICATION, SUBTERFUGE, ETC.

"To test his objections as to their correctness or better to instruct himself in Catholic doctrine was not a matter of need to one who...looked upon lying as a serviceable expedient." (2)

"If Luther wanted to set up an argument against 'monkery' from baptism, he had perforce to lie, for the true Catholic doctrine gave him no foothold. And he did simply lie, and it was just he, who, like no other before him, debased the dignity of baptism." (2)

"To cover his own lies and his own contradictions, he accuses the Church of lying and of contradiction." (2)

"His [Luther's] sources, however, are very suspicious, for in part he fabricated them himself." (2)

"Luther also exempted himself from a literal interpretation of the commandment against lying, for he publicly averred that it was perfectly acceptable to 'tell a good thumping lie' if it (supposedly) benefited Christianity." (Crocker, "Triumph: The Power and the Glory of the Catholic Church")

"He who tells a falsehood and lies, does not afterwards know what he had earlier asserted. Thus it was with Luther. He himself set up his trap and was caught in it." (2)

"...in [Luther's] hatred of, and warfare against, the Church, he unscrupulously assumes the blame for his immeasurable distortions of Catholic doctrine and for the gravest calumnies against Catholic antiquity. He did this when he held 'everything (!) to be permissible against the insidiousness and wickedness of Popedom, for the salvation of one's soul,' even lies of utility, which, particularly from this point of view, he allows and defends." (2)

"Luther...often defended the permissibility of lies of utility." (2) [Refresher: "Lying lips are an abomination to the LORD, but those who are truthful are his delight." (Prov. 12:22)]

"Luther made use of sophistries, distortions, and lies in order to set hated celibacy free. This was the aim of the conspiracy upon which he entered with Melanchthon. He knew well that if he adhered to the truth he could not accomplish his purpose." (2)

"Luther does not stop at sophistry. The [so-called] Reformer betrays his followers into becoming hypocrites. He counsels restrictio mentalis (mental reservation) in its worst sense of dissimulation, in which he himself was a master." (2)

"It is not another but Luther who drives the monks into hypocrisy, into lying, into deception. One thing is said with the lips, another is meant in the heart within... [A]ccording to Luther, a secret 'yes' may be, aye, must be an open 'no,' and that it doesn't signify if one compasses a good strong lie for something better and for the sake of the Christian Church..." (2)

"...[Luther] is always falsifying Catholic teaching." (2)

"It has repeatedly struck our attention that Luther was a master in sophistry. His talent was of service to him in its formulation and after his apostasy, in his warfare against the Church, he made use of it to deceive others and to tear them away from her." (2)

"Catholic opponents...were unable to draw enough attention to Luther's cunning and lying." (2)

"Luther, when he called [St.] Thomas the inventor of 'monastic baptism,' either deceived his readers or he only evidenced his ignorance. Likely he did both. Moreover he knew the 'Vitae Patrum,' he knew [St.] Bernard's work 'de praecepto et dispensatione,' both of which he otherwise frequently cites. Why, then, these subterfuges of his, and, besides, a wholly erroneous exposition of the doctrine itself?... As Luther shrank from no means, if it availed to fight the Church, so did he stop at nothing to belittle [St.] Thomas..." (2)

An example of one of Luther's lies about Catholic doctrine: "The Papists hold marriage to be out-and-out impurity and sin, in which one cannot serve God." (2)

"His [Luther's] insidious character, with which and against which he never busied himself, least of all after his apostasy, entered essentially into his deceptions in respect to St. Bernard, his perversions with regard to the essence of the vows and to the form of profession, his sophisms...his counsel to priests and religious to put their own mental construction on their vows, as he proposes, and the rest. What was quite his own he ascribed to the Church. Naturally he then says: Everything is allowed against the deception and wickedness of the Papal chair, therefore also a good, stout lie; for if this was allowed for the sake of his Church, as we heard him say, it was also above all permitted against its adversary. Of what is a person not capable who takes lies of necessity, lies of utility, helping lies upon his conscience? He will use them as his most powerful allies against his enemies. The apostates from the orders and from the Church made and still make use of them. 'To the first of the devil's weapons belongs that one which is called a lie, which he adorns with the sacred name of God, of Christ, and of the Church, and precisely with which he damns the truth and seeks to turn it into a lie.' Thus runs Luther's own admission. It is no wonder, then, that Duke George, on the occasion of the Pack affair, described Luther, December 19, 1528, as 'the most coldblooded liar that ever got among us.' 'We must say and write of him that the recreant monk lies to our face like a despairing, dishonorable, perjured scoundrel.' 'We have hitherto not found in the Scriptures that Christ used so open and deliberate a liar in the apostolic office, allowing him to preach the gospel.' Others who knew Luther spoke to the same effect.' I [the priestly author of the work] also shall venture to say the same of him without reserve. To that I am determined by my exhaustive and wholly unbiased studies of Luther." (2)

"It is significant for the 'Evangelical Church' that in it this wholly corrupt treatise [of Luther], filled with sophisms, contradictions, lies, and calumnies, enjoys so much repute, and that its confession, the Augustana, is built up on this work, so far as its contents are concerned. He who makes free and agile use of guile and lying, like Luther, verifying, as rarely another did, the proverb he quoted: 'He who willingly lies, must also lie when he tells the truth'; he to whom hardly a means is too evil to procure the admission among others of his propositions against the Church - is not such a one also capable, if it answers his purpose, of lying about his own earlier life?" (2)

"If we put everything together, we see, as a result amounting almost to certainty, that Luther's later utterances on his one-time immoderate self-chastisements and on the purpose he had had in performing them, belong to the intentional lies of utility, which, not even excepting big ones, he holds to be permissible and which he defends for the weal of his 'church' and of his doctrine." (2)

"...[Luther] shrank from no means of calumniating the Church and of making her hated, so that thereby his own doctrine might be exalted!" (2)

"It was precisely in respect to the Evangelical counsels that Luther, in his book on the vows, rendered himself guilty of the greatest contradictions and sophisms. Never in his life a theologically trained and disciplined scholar, he exceeded all bounds and bearing after his apostasy. Moreover, he knew that his victims, whether those already apostatized or the dissolute monks in the monasteries, were concerned not in contradictions or sophisms but rather in having the rejection of all restraints and their wiving made plausible. Luther who was burning with carnal lust during the composition of his book at the Wartburg, no longer observed his contradictions and sophisms." (2)

LUTHER HAD A VIRULENT HATRED OF THE CHURCH AND RELIGIOUS ORDERS

"But, from 1520 on, what means did Luther employ against the Church, the orders, and the priesthood? Words of contempt, abuse, calumnies were with him the order of the day." (2)

"U. Zasius had already said: 'I must first say that Luther with brazen shamelessness interprets the whole Scripture of the Old and New Testament, from the first book of the Bible to the end, against popes and priests, as if God, from the beginning of the world, had had no other business than to thunder against the priesthood." (2)

"To him priests and monks are 'devils in disguise,' 'coarse, fat *sses, adorned with red and brown (i.e. violet) birettas, like the sow.'" (2)

"Why, I will clothe an *ss with such a frock, gird him with a rope, shave a tonsure on him, stand him in a corner, and he shall also fast and celebrate (in honor of) the saints." (Luther) (2)

"It was this vulgar, ribald character that, as early as 1521, inspired the 'Reformer' to utter the counsel: 'I consider it the best that, in the future, the priesthood be called not priests but shavelings ('Plattentrager,' wearers of a bald pate), and that the useless folk be driven out of the land. Of what use to us is the shaveling-gang, priests neither spiritually nor corporeally? And what need have we of them, since we ourselves are all corporeal, spiritual, and every kind of priests? Like alien useless guests, they gobble our bread. Therefore out with them, out with the rascals'. Hence, in 1540, he could say in his foul manner: 'Where, in the long run, will the Papists get monks and priests? Here in Wittenberg there are many students, but I do not believe a single one would let himself be anointed and hold his mouth open for the Pope to void his dirt into it.' (The original German here, as in many other places, is too vulgar to be tolerated in its corresponding equivalent in English. -- Translator's note.)" (2) *[Note: Translator's note above appears in the source publication.]*

"A ribald, whose only concern is to make a whole state of life ridiculous, must needs have recourse to lies, if he is to succeed. For, that one cannot and may not condemn a whole state of life, Luther himself in his better days proved with drastic effect. Now what a higgledy-piggledy of ribaldry, trifling, and lying do not the above-cited words of Luther contain? We find him therein in his own true humor to deliver priesthood and monasticism over to the mockery of the world and to do everything to vex the hated Papists. 'The while they, in their judgment, are triumphing over one of my heresies, I, in the meantime, will produce a new one.' It is that humor in which he acted on the principle of making a 'counter-play', of doing the precise opposite of the 'mad laws of the Pope', even of scheming what scandal he might set up, in order to anger them and at the same time to [supposedly] please God!" (2)

"In his warfare against the orders (especially the Franciscan and the Dominican), Luther desired to deal a blow to the Papacy. He knew well that precisely the orders, especially the mendicant, and among them again the Franciscans and the Dominicans, are the most powerful auxiliary forces of the Church, as Luther himself confesses. To hit the Church most effectively, he had to make an end of the orders. This could succeed only if, on the one side, the religious could be brought to violate their vows and to abandon their monasteries and, if on the other hand, they could be made hateful to the people, who clung more to the religious, especially the mendicants, than to the pastoral clergy." (2)

"'Happy are you that, by honorable marriage, you have overcome that unclean celibacy, which, partly on account of constant s*xual desire and partly immundis fluxibus, is to be condemned...I hold marriage to he a paradise.' Thus did he [Luther] write as he was about to compose his treatise on the monastic vows, after at the same time acknowledging that in the Wartburg he 'was exposed to a thousand devils' and that he came 'frequently to fall'. Some months previous, before he had published his theses on the vows, Luther writes: 'I also wish to set celibacy free, as the Gospel requires, but how to accomplish that I do not yet sufficiently know' But if he was already convinced that the Gospel demanded the liberty of celibacy, how could he say that he did not yet know how to bring it about that celibacy might be set free? All he needed to do was to step forward with those words of the Gospel which in his opinion demanded the liberty of celibacy, and the thing was done. But therein lay the difficulty. Well did Luther know that the Gospel, the sacred Scripture, was not on his side. So he considered how he might get it on his side. This he did in the same wise as in the case of the utterances of [St.] Bernard, of the constitutions of his Order, of the teachings of the Church, namely, by falsification and contradictions, by trickery and sophistries. On this head I need not in any particular manner waste further words. We find the evidences at every crook and turn. 'Luther is ashamed of no lie,' wrote the Dominican John Mensing of his time. He made no scruple of misleading priests and monks into dissimulation, into restrictio mentalis (mental reservation) in the worse sense of the word, and finally of expressly declaring a lie permissible. It is evident what one can expect of such a man and what one can think of him. He falsifies and distorts ideas, and then assails the caricature he has made, as Catholic doctrine." (2)

"First Luther distorted the doctrine on the counsels and vows and their relation to the commandments. He did this in such wise as to make the vows appear to be contrary to faith. At the same time he aroused carnal lust in the dissolute monks, and especially the nuns, mirrored to them the impossibility of resistance, and the uselessness of prayer, which they had neglected anyhow, and deceived them with the thought that God could not even help them to be continent, since He had instituted marriage as a remedy against 'impossibility.' He represented the violation of the vows as a work pleasing to God, marriage as God's commandment. His conclusion was: 'It is wholly and completely evident that your vows are null, not permitted, godless, running counter to the Gospel. Therefore one may not even debate whether you took them with a devout or with a godless intention, since it is certain that you vowed godless things. Consequently you must put your trust in the Gospel, abandon your vows, and turn back to Christian liberty.' Those who were ripe for their fall heard this gladly." (2)

"Yet he [Luther] spoke in a manner entirely different, before satanic hatred of the Church, whose ruin he had sworn, guided him. Above I have already quoted his words out of the year 1516, to the effect that religious could be the happiest, the most blessed (of people), if they wished, i.e., if they lived like true religious. According to even Luther's admission, therefore, the religious life was able to afford true satisfaction and peace of soul. As a true religious, one has but 'to take upon one's self the sweet cross of Christ, obedience according to the rule, to follow His will and Him whom the heart desires, not like a cross that the thief on the left bore with murmuring, but like the one which St. Andrew received...The mouth of truth promised you it will be light and joyous, when He spoke: 'my yoke is sweet and my burden light, and you shall find rest to your souls.' Believe those who have experienced it. If there is a paradise in this world, it is either in the cloister or in studying.' Such also was once the judgment of Luther, when he still grasped the idea of the religious life; but now he held marriage to be paradise, as we saw above, i.e., the giving up of the monastic life by the violation of the vows and by wiving. For he was already mired. He had fallen away from the idea of the true religious. Through his own fault he now found everything that was once a pleasure to him burdensome, and he cast it off for the gratification of the lusts of the flesh." (2)

"There is nothing to be done without the people. If they were fond of the orders, they would also be fond of the Church, whose destruction Luther had sworn. It was therefore necessary to cause the Church to be hated by the people. The means to this end varied according to circumstances." (2)

"Luther bluntly calls the monks, nuns, and priests, 'belly-servers,' 'greedy guts.' 'Nasty sows are they altogether.' In the Tabletalk the language is even worse." (2)

"He [Luther] calls the Catholic celibates ...'a class of men most abandoned to libidinousness, wh*rishness, and adultery, who day and night only dream of their lustful diversions, and imagine what they would do, if such privilege were granted to them (as to the patriarchs), so that they could exchange consorts every night, and could sport with them according to the flames and ardor of the flesh, as they sport with their wh*res.'" (2)

"From Luther's lips the people had already heard the calumny that the papistical doing of good works took place irrespective of Christ, that it aimed to effect salvation, attain to forgiveness of sin, and to merit heaven without Christ. Since therefore this doing of works was directed against the Savior, Who anyhow had abrogated all law, there was no state of life that gave better occasion for Luther's blustering against Catholic holiness-by-works, as he called it, than the religious state with its laws. The more he piled up the 'holy-by-works' in it, the more merry and urgent his blustering became. Consequently it did not abash him in the slightest degree at such an opportunity and for the purpose named, to depict all, or most, or many religious of his time who lived strictly according to their rule, as holy by works, and self-justified. On the contrary, that served him before the people for the conclusion: they all, because being deniers of Christ, belong to the devil." (2)

"To make the Church and her monasticism the victim of contempt, no means was too evil for Luther." (2)

"Luther and his following fed on the lie that the Pope sets up, 'without the word of God, new orders and new modes of life, ascribing to them the same as to Christ, namely, that by them eternal salvation may be obtained.' 'When I have reached the judgment that there is nothing that justifies before God, save the blood of Christ, I at once conclude: therefore are the statutes of the popes, the rules of the fathers a leading astray.' This is reason enough, he opines, 'to have all monasteries razed to the ground.' And so by force of arms after all? It was his wish." (2)

"Nevertheless only a few lines farther on he urges that 'the secular authorities and the nobility should bring their regular power to bear upon the case as a matter of duty (i.e., to set upon the Papacy and the priesthood), each prince and lord in his country. For, that which is done by regular power is not to be held as an uprising!' And so the secular authorities, i.e., the hand and power of men, are to destroy the Papal ecclesiastical state! Such was Luther's fundamental view from the time of his apostasy until his death. 'All monasteries' he says in 1523, 'and all cathedrals and similar abominations in the holy place are to be wholly annihilated or abandoned, since they persuade men into open dishonor of the blood of Christ and of the faith, into putting trust in their own works in seeking their salvation, which is nothing else but denying the Lord, Who purchased us, as Peter says.'

In 1545 he wishes only some monasteries to remain - as an object of shame. All the others are to be razed... 'I would that all the pulpits in the world,' he preached several years earlier, 'lay in fire with monasteries, foundations, churches, hermitages, and chapels, and that all were idle dust and ashes, because of the horrible misleading of poor souls.' The great misleader of Germany, Luther, dares to write this!" (2)

"More important and wholly pertinent to the matter is what Luther writes in the same year, 1521, in his treatise on the monastic vows: 'Because of this abomination alone, (the wounding of filial charity by the religious), I would that all monasteries were blotted out, done away with, and uprooted, as they should be too...if only God would exterminate them to the very root, as He did Sodom and Gomorrah, with fire and sulphur, so that not even the memory of them might be left!' In 1529, he likewise urges that 'we should destroy the Pope's idolatry and false divine service and abuses.' 'We must do with the Papacy what Moses did with the golden calf - annihilate it into dust. God is so hostile to the (Papal) divine service, that it is not His will that a single atom of it should be left over.' Foundations and monasteries, writes Luther the next year, 'should be smashed into smithereens.' In 1531, he wishes hell-fire upon the heads of Kaiser, King, Pope, and Papists, or that the Papacy and all its appurtenances may go into the abyss of hell. In 1532: 'Oh, how much have I yet to preach and to talk that the Pope with his triple crown and with the cardinals and bishops, priests and monks who follow him...may go down to the devil.'" (2)

"What he [Luther] said in general, 1540, 'We shall accomplish nothing against the Turks unless we smite them with the priests at the right time, and hurl them even unto death,' was leveled in particular against the religious. Luther forthwith took up every anecdote, every suspicion against them as facts, e.g., that they were the instigators of the incendiary fires of that time. He did this that he might vent his deadly hatred upon them in the reminder: 'If the matter comes to light, there will be nothing left but in common to take arms against all monks and priests; and I will go along, too, for one should strike the rascals dead...' 'If I had all the Franciscan monks together in one house, I would set the house on fire. For the kernel is gone from the monks, only the chaff is still at hand. So into the fire with them!' And what of that? The religious 'are not worth being called human beings; they should not so much as be called swine.'" (2)

According to Luther, "Monks are always priests of the devil, for they keep up a vain devilish doctrine." (2)

"Luther's gospel with its fundamental thought, justification and forgiveness of sin by faith alone, led both theoretically and practically to the consequent proposition: therefore all the good works and everything we impose upon ourselves and do, are useless for salvation. Nay more, he who considers works as a necessary factor on the way of salvation exercises them 'without the blood of Christ,' consequently denies the Savior and Redeemer, puts his own work in the place of Christ, and is 'drowned' in a service of works. In consequence of this, Luther had to condemn, as justification by works and holiness by works, not only all Christian life in general, but above all its religious life. There is no life that possesses so many works and exercises as the religious state. And since a religious binds himself to this life by vow, the 'Reformer' naturally came to hold the religious life as a seat of unbelief, a den of cut-throats, a life accursed." (2)

LUTHER PROMOTED A DANGEROUS 'CHRISTIAN LIBERTY'/FREE LICENSE

"When from the beginning the people heard celibacy, not only as it was observed here and there in practice, but in general, decried as 'impure, godless, and abominable,' they held that to apply to chastity as well, the more so as they had to hear from the same lips that the s*xual instinct is irresistible and that, to the Papists, celibacy and chastity meant the same thing. Once the heart has simply lost its regard for chastity, conjugal chastity dies out also, and there is an end to the dignity of matrimony. But woe if there are still added to that doctrines making for the dissolution of the marriage bond, affirming Christian liberty, denying free will, and asserting the nothingness of works, etc., as Luther gradually developed them. As a matter of fact the 'Reformer' wrote in 1523: 'Christian liberty makes it possible that all outer things are free before God and a Christian can use them as he will; he may accept them or let them pass. And Paul adds: 'with God,' i.e., as much as matters between you and God. For you render no service to God because you marry or stay single, become a servant, free, this or that, or eat this or that;

again you do Him no annoyance nor sin if you omit or put off one of those things. Finally, you do not owe it to God to do anything but to believe and confess (Him). In all other things He sets you unbound and free, so that you may do as you will, without any peril to conscience; nay more, so that, on His own account, He asked no questions whether you let your wife go, ran from the Lord, and kept no covenant. For what is it to Him that you do or do not do such things?' According to Luther, then, God makes no inquiry about us, whether we are wh*ring or murdering. This of itself does not concern Him! Of the contradiction in which he thus entangled himself, Luther was unaware. If God has joined a married couple together - which Luther must admit on the authority of Christ's words: 'What God hath joined together, let no man put asunder,' (Matt. 19:6) - how is it conceivable that an adulterer, as such, is not to be thought sinning against God?" (2)

LUTHER'S FOLLOWERS JOINED HIM FOR 'CARNAL LIBERTY'

"[Luther] knew how his followers lived and that, for the most part, they had gone over to him only for the sake of carnal liberty." (2)

"Piercing beneath the motivations of Luther's followers, Erasmus saw that for them, the overthrow of the terrestrial power of the Church was motivated by a greed for Church property and a lust to break the bonds of celibacy. Lutheranism had 'but two objects at heart,' Erasmus said, 'money and women.'" (Crocker, "Triumph: The Power and the Glory of the Catholic Church")

"In truth, who were those who had apostatized from their orders to Luther? By those who were left, who knew them well by years of association with them, they were called the rabble, the chaff; they were knaves in the sense of wh*remongers, of whom the Dominican, Johann Mensing, gives judgment: 'Alas, knaves are knaves, in whatever state of life, profession, or order they may be. And we hope that, where hitherto they have been in the Papacy, they will nearly all have escaped and run over to Luther. Would to God, Who perhaps will clean up His threshing-floor and separate the wheat from the chaff, that he (Luther) now had them all, who wish to do no good among us! For it is manifest that no one (not gulled out of simplicity) takes refuge in the Lutheran sect to become more pious and of better mind, but that he may live free and unpunished and without reserve do all that he pleases.'" (2)

"As is evident, it was genuine good fortune for the Church, to get rid of these unclean subjects and to have the atmosphere purified. But so much the more impure did it become within the domain of Lutheranism. For those unhappy apostates did not go over to Luther to do penance and in the future to bring themselves under subjection. On the contrary, it was just Luther's doctrine on the impossibility of resisting carnal lust that attracted them. Their longing centered on a free life and a wife! Those, especially the secular priests, who had already been living in immorality, (which Luther and his fellows had so often charged against them whilst they were still under the Papacy) went over to him, not to put away their concubines, but to be able to continue living with them with a conscience freed by Luther. Hence the great swarm of concubinaries who swelled Luther's society. They went over to Luther, as we heard Mensing say, to live free and unpunished, and without reserve to do what they pleased, or as was written by Usingen, Luther's former professor, to whom Luther once had so commended the religious life: 'All who wish to lead a dissolute life join the Evangelicals.' What greater encouragement, besides, could have been given to them than Luther's opinion, expressed as early as 1520, that the Christian could commit as many sins as he liked, could not lose his salvation, so long as he was not without faith, etc.? Was it not the right gospel and glad tidings to those godless souls, when they heard from the lips of the father of the 'Evangelical Reformation' that sin does not separate from God? If 'you acknowledge the Lamb, which beareth the sins of the world, sin cannot tear you from Him, even though you do wh*rishness a thousand times a day, or deal as many death-blows.' 'One must sin as long as we are in this existence. This life is not the dwelling place of justice.' A complacent trust in the forgiveness of sin through Christ does everything! No wonder his former superior could write to him in the year 1522: 'Your case is continually spoken of and extolled by those who frequent the wh*re-houses.'" (2)

"The others, on the contrary, received from the father of the 'Evangelical Reformation' the wholly unevangelical encouragement: 'Be a sinner and sin stoutly, but more stoutly trust in Christ, the conqueror of sin.' In the face of such subjects and of such cheering exhortations, what sort of organization could arise, especially when they further heard that the moral law, as such, did not concern Christians, that every man by nature, even in Christianity, is at heart at least, an adulterer? Add to this that these subjects, Luther included, lived their lives without prayer, without fasting, without chastisement..." (2)

DESPITE HIS EARLIER VOWS, LUTHER PUBLICLY PRACTICED IMMORALITY

"...nobody doubted Luther's too pronounced intimacy with women before his wiving." (2)

"One needs not therefore urge the words written August 10, 1528 by Joachim von der Heyden to Catherine Bora, to the effect that she had betaken herself to Wittenberg like a dancing girl and had lived with Luther in open and flagrant immorality before taking him as her husband." (2)

OUT OF SPITE, LUTHER BROKE HIS VOWS TO MARRY A FORMER NUN

"In August, 1525, [Luther] writes that he took the Bora woman to wife out of contempt for the Papists, and that, if he can, he will do more to spite them and that they may confess the word. On January 5, 1526, writing to Marquard Schuldorp, who had married his sister's daughter, he gives expression to these hair-raising words, which manifest the state of his soul to the whole world: 'I also took a nun to wife, however I might have been able to arrange and had no particular reason except that I did it to spite the devil with his scabs, the big Jacks, princes, and bishops, who are like to be downright crazy because ecclesiastics are to be free. And I would gladly set up more scandal, if only I knew of something more that pleased God and annoyed them. For thereby do I vent my feeling at their raging against the Gospel that they are angered, and I do not care and always keep on and do it all the more, the more they do not want it." (2)

MORE ON LUTHER & HIS MARRIAGE

"By this marriage I have made myself so mean and despicable that I hope the angels will laugh and all devils weep." (Luther) (2)

Luther is fully deceived: "He further states that God had wonderfully thrown him into marriage with the nun...and that one must confess his wiving to be a 'work, a thing of God'." (2)

LUTHER'S MISBEHAVIOR

"Luther said in a letter to Bora, July 2, 1540: 'I gorge like a Bohemian and guzzle like a German.'" (2)

Luther admittedly was "consumed by the fires of [his] unbridled flesh" and "consumed by the flesh and by lasciviousness" (De Wette, 2, 22)

"I burn with a thousand flames in my unsubdued flesh: I feel myself carried on with a rage towards women that approaches madness. I, who ought to be fervent in spirit, am only fervent in impurity." (Luther, Table Talk)

"'Luther,' as his associate Melanchthon writes, 'was an exceedingly wanton man'" (2)

Luther was admittedly 'lazy in prayer': "On Sept. 9, 1521, he writes to Spalatin: 'Poor man that I am, I grow cold in spirit. I am still snoring on, and am lazy in prayer.'" (2)

"...Luther was never a man of prayer. In at least his better period, however, he understood its great utility. After his apostasy, he lost even the notion at times, and he was obliged repeatedly to acknowledge that, under the Pope, he and his following had been more frequent, more zealous, more earnest, and more diligent in prayer than now; they were now much more remiss than under the Papacy. However much he might otherwise speak of prayer, in himself it was largely hypocrisy." (2)

"He, Melanchthon, and his associates had often rebuked him on account of his buffoonery." (2)

"...we see him [Luther], from 1520 on, treating the gravest affairs of the soul, decisive for time and eternity, with incredible levity and buffoonery." (2)

"...[Luther] gradually got to the proposition that concupiscence is irresistible, and then, in much grosser fashion, saddled his own unchastity upon all." (2)

"Is one to seek Luther's 'earnest sense,' his 'profoundly earnest spirit,' the evidence 'that he was too sober for trifling,' in the fact that, from the beginning of his warfare against the Church and the theologians, he takes pains to make his opponents ridiculous and to expose them to mockery?" (2)

"Luther, who, as we saw, had no mind for tomfoolery four years before, was now pleased with it in his warfare against the Church and made use of its antics to ridicule Pope, bishops, priests, and monks." (2)

"Like another Don Quixote, the 'Reformer' fights a phantom, in order then to blare himself the victor. In the end, he, who had broken his vows and had misled others to do the same, assumes the role of great gravity: 'The word and the commandment of God stands for eternity. It suffers no jest nor perversion and distortion.' He perverts and distorts everything. He does it intentionally, and the very ones whose teachings he has perverted and distorted, he censures for perversion and distortion!" (2)

"I cannot deny I am more violent than is becoming; since my opponents know this, they ought not to excite the dog." (Luther) (2)

"Almost all condemn in me my mordacity." (Luther) (2)

"Once Luther's setting forth the abuses in the Church proceeded from the endeavors which he in common with many of his contemporaries made to fight against degeneration for a better condition. Now, since 1520, their setting forth was solely a means of agitation with him, in order to make the hated Papists the object of universal mockery and to divert eyes from the far worse corruption, the boundless immorality, and the unchristian life of his own house." (2)

"...Luther hid for a year in a castle in Wartburg, Germany, where he lost himself in massive bouts of eating and drinking, pausing occasionally to wrestle with the devil in a paroxysm of delusion, engaging him in battle by f*rt. He also translated the Bible into German, rewriting passages so that they expounded Lutheran doctrine - for instance by adding the word 'alone' after the word 'faith' in Romans 3:28. His daily prayers were rather unique as well. In Luther's words, 'I am unable to pray without at the same time cursing. If I am prompted to say: 'hallowed be Thy name,' I must add: 'cursed, damned, outraged be the name of the papists.' If I am prompted to say: 'Thy Kingdom come,' I must perforce add: 'cursed, damned, destroyed be the papacy.'" (Crocker, "Triumph: The Power and the Glory of the Catholic Church")

"The older Luther got to be, the more outrageous he was. We hear from his lips: 'Nuns are so called from a Germanism: for that is what castrated sows are denominated, as monks from horses (i.e., castrated ones.) But they are not yet healed. They have to wear breeches as well as other people.' What vulgarity!" (2)

"As the apothecary was applying the tube [to Luther's dead body], he heard several loud winds discharged into the clyster-bag. In consequence of his intemperate eating and drink, Luther's body was wholly bloated with cachectic humors." (2)

"Looking over the...[material discussed], we get worse than a bad impression of Luther's principles, demeanor, and character. We hit, not upon a man who even half deserved the title of a reformer, but upon an agitator, an overthrower, to whom no sophistry is too audacious, no artifice too bad, no lie too strong, no calumny too great, to justify his apostasy from the Church and from his own earlier principles. The entire Catholic doctrine on the counsels, on the vows, in a word, on the whole religious state was distorted by him and made contemptible before the whole world. The hearts of the religious were thus to be estranged from their state, to be incited to the violation of their vows and to marriage, or, if they had already ventured upon that step, to be confirmed in it. Luther does not shrink even from giving himself the lie by the statutes of his own Order, to ascribe words and views to himself as a young monk which he had never entertained; he does not disdain to falsify Catholic doctrine, even to hold up to his contemporaries as universally valid, propositions which not a soul either then or earlier had even thought of. The better to draw priests and religious, already decadent, into his toils, he represents to them the 'impossibility' of resisting their s*xual instinct, and marriage as a conscientious duty. And what principles he developed on the latter, i.e., on marriage! The more his following increased, the more boldly and audaciously he took his stand." (2)

- - - - - - - - - - - - - - - - -

SOME RESULTS OF LUTHER'S TEACHINGS...

- - - - - - - - - - - - - - - - -

LUTHER'S TEACHINGS ADMITTEDLY RESULTED IN CONTEMPT FOR THE HOLY EUCHARIST

"People have now so little esteem for the Holy Sacrament of the Body and Blood of our Lord...it is as if there was nothing on earth that they were less in want of." (Luther) (1)

"Formerly under the Pope, when we were forced and urged to receive the Sacrament, we went in crowds...now...our behavior towards it is as disgusting and shameless, that it is as if we were not human beings (still less Christians), but only sticks and stones, that stand in no need of it." (Luther) (1)

LUTHER'S TEACHINGS LEAD TO PERSECUTION OF PRIESTS

"The complaints of the priests in Eberlin von Gunsburg are wholly in accord with Luther's words: 'A priest absolutely dares not show his tonsure any longer, for the commoner is quite heated against the priesthood. In their case a mountain is made of a mole-hill, and the anger of God breaks over them. And all that do the priests an injury get to thinking they are thereby doing God a service.' It is a wonder, it was said, the people do not stone them to death. 'Before forty years pass, the very dogs will void their urine on us priests.'" (2)

LUTHER'S TEACHINGS ADMITTEDLY DRIED UP CHARITY

"Formerly, under the Pope people gave very largely indeed and beyond measure...then they gave in heaps for they looked...upon the reward...But now that with the light of the Gospel [of Luther] we are told nothing about our merits, nobody is willing to give and to help." (Luther) (1)

"Formerly, when we served the Devil under Popery, everybody was merciful and kind; then they gave with both hands, joyfully and with great devotion... Now that we ought to be merciful, to give willingly, and to show ourselves thankful to God for the Holy Gospel [of Luther] nobody is willing to give, but only to take." (Luther) (1)

FRUITS OF LUTHER'S TEACHING INCLUDED WIDESPREAD DRUNKENNESS

"[Drunkenness] has spread...among the youth...so that now the greater part of the finest, most talented young men (especially among the nobility and at Court), undermine their health, their body and their life..." (Luther) (1)

"We have now got so far that coarse vices, excessive drinking, rioting are no longer looked upon as a disgrace, but...drunkenness must now be called hilarity." (Luther) (1)

"Drunkenness has now, I am sorry to say, come down upon us...like a deluge." (Luther) (1)

"The people are like pigs, so to speak, dead and buried in constant drunkenness." (Luther) (1)

"Sarcerius finds a chief cause of the prevalent wh*rishness and many adulteries of his time in the circumstance that 'there was neither limit nor measure to drinking and gormandizing.' It is justly said: a drunken man, an unchaste man; a drunken woman, an unchaste woman. And Luther had it: 'a drunken sow cannot have Christian life.' Unfortunately, however, it was just under Luther's gospel that in Germany, the demon of drink, though he did not come into existence, nevertheless attained his growth. 'Every country must have its own devil... Our German devil will be a good wine-bibber and must be named Guzzle (Sauf), being so dry and thirsty that he cannot be refreshed with such great guzzling of wine and beer. Guzzle will remain an almighty idol among us Germans, and he acts like the ocean and like dropsy. The ocean does not get full on all the waters that flow into it; dropsy gets thirstier and worse by drinking.' That the 'man of God' was a child of the times in the matter of drinking, as in others, has already been noted. Even his father was given to drunkenness, but it made him jolly, not rabid, as it did Luther's sister's son, Hans Polner, pastor of Jessen. But Luther did not want everyone to follow him in his potations...Soon there was talk in Germany of an Order of Guzzlers." (2)

LUTHER'S TEACHINGS LED TO ADULTERY / POLYGAMY / LACK OF CHASTITY

"The lewd and adulterous life, the contempt of the marriage state at that time, are consequences of Luther's course and teachings." (2)

"From such a state of affairs, it was only a step farther to polygamy. Several of these apostles of the flesh did go to that length, inasmuch as, faithful to their principles, they allowed, at times, two and three wives. Some, indeed, of these fallen priests and monks themselves had several women at the same time. Later it was their own leader who accounted polygamy among the ultimate and highest things of Christian liberty; he would not forbid 'that one take more wives than one, for,' he says, 'it is not contrary to Holy Writ.' 'Only to avoid scandal and for the sake of decency one should not do it.'" (2)

"Luther's doctrine on faith was also a contributing factor to adultery. The Protestant rector, J. Eivius, writes in 1547 'If you are an adulterer, say the preachers, or one given to wh*rishness,...only believe and you will be saved. You need not let yourself be frightened by law, for Christ fulfilled it and made satisfaction for man... Such talking misleads to a godless life,' etc. Such was also the case when a common man heard Luther preaching: 'No work is evil enough to be able to damn a man (only) disbelief damns us. If one falls into adultery, that action does not damn him'; he only evidences his fall from faith." (2)

"One who returned to the Mother Church, the Lutheran Professor Fr. Staphylus, wrote in 1562: 'As long as marriage was regarded as a sacrament, chastity and honorable marriage-life were held dear and of worth, but since the people have read in Luther's books that the marriage state is a human invention, Luther's counsels...have at once been carried out to such a degree that there is absolutely more chastity and honor in the married state in Turkey than among our Evangelicals in Germany.'" (2)

"The most distinguished of the Danish theologians, Nicholas Hemming, thus expressed himself in 1562:

'Once modesty was the most precious treasure of the young women, but now in dress and demeanor they betray all shamelessness.' Indeed, 'when unchaste pleasure has brought them to their downfall, or they live otherwise in shameless licentiousness, they become so bold that they allege Luther's law as a pretext; a chaste, continent life is impossible to man, the gratification of the s*xual instinct is as necessary as food and drink.'" (2)

"Whilst the 'Reformer' is seeking to rid himself of one blame, he incurs another. Duke George of Saxony complains of the increase of adulteries in consequence of Luther's teaching. This teaching was to blame that man took more than one wife, inasmuch as they 'absconded to parts unknown, and let themselves be given other wives. A number of women do the same. Hence there is no end nor limit to the runaways of husbands and wives.' But this occurred not only after emigration to 'parts unknown,' but in the very place and spot, and generally in Germany; it even, or rather naturally, was rampant in Luther's own district, where he was born, where he died, in the county of Mansfeld. Touching this matter the superintendent of the place wrote: 'In many places there is fearful wh*rishness and adultery going on, and so common have these vices become that a number do not consider them sins.' 'Hence there is everywhere a disorderly and scandalous fashion at the beginning and carrying out of marriage, so that the holy marriage state is dishonored and trampled under foot.' 'And thus almost everywhere there are now secret betrothals, aye, one is engaged to more than one person.' 'Of adultery, unchastity, and incest there is no end.'" (2)

"Now who was the spiritual father of that generation? Was it not Luther? Who invited priests, religious, and nuns to violate their God-sworn vows? Was it not he? But that was paving the way to the violation of the matrimonial vows as well, and to general unfaithfulness, about which Luther later so complained, without making himself responsible therefore. He himself, by his wiving in 1525, only set a seal on his infidelity to God." (2)

LUTHER'S TEACHING RESULTED IN LOWER MORALITY

"As soon as our Gospel began...decency...and modesty were done away with, and everybody wished to be perfectly free to do whatever he liked." (Luther) (1)

"After one Devil (Popery) has been driven out of us, seven worse ones have come down upon us" (Luther) (1)

"In all classes frivolity and every kind of vice, sin, and disgrace are now much greater than formerly." (Luther) (1)

"The more and the longer we preach, the worse matters grow." (Luther) (1)

"...men are now more avaricious, unmerciful, impure, insolent...than formerly under the Pope.'" (Luther) (1)

"About a year before his death, Luther confesses: 'We are living in Sodom and Babylon...everything is daily getting worse." (1)

LUTHER'S WAS A DOWNWARD REFORM, WHICH IN SOME PLACES WAS ACCOMPLISHED BY FORCE

"Lutheranism now began to be intruded into various places by force of arms. Luther saw the seeds of religious dissolution already at work. His health was broken and his spirit, save as against Rome. He entertained grave doubts about the efficacy of his work. The reform he saw to be a reform downwards. Public morals were at a lower grade than they had been before. 'Since we began to preach our doctrine,' he said in his pulpit at Wittenberg in 1532, 'the world has grown daily worse, more impious, and more shameless. Men are now beset by legions of devils, and, while enjoying the full light of the Gospel, are more avaricious, more impure and repulsive, than of old under the Papacy. Peasants, burghers, and noblesmen of all degrees, the highest as well as the lowest- are all alike slaves to avarice, drunkenness, gluttony, and impurity, and given over to shameful excesses and abominable passions.' 'Let us go from this Sodom,' he wrote to Catharine in 1545, and quitted Wittenberg in disgust, only returning at the demand of the elector and of the university. At Eisleben he died shortly after delivering a most violent sermon against the Jews." (4)

"In a word, the entire concubinage of the fifteenth century and its congeneric continuation in the sixteenth, with all its abominations, pale before the

78

doings and the teachings of the fallen priests and monks who, in the third decade of the sixteenth century, had branched off from the old movement. 'Monasticism now truly lies stretched out on the ground' writes Erasmus, who certainly was not less than edified by the earlier condition, 'but if the monks had only put off their vices with their cowls!' ... 'It seems to me there is a new kind of monks arising, much more wicked than the former, bad as these were. It is folly to substitute evil for evil, but it is madness to exchange the bad for even worse.' This, according to Luther, is what heretics do generally. 'They exchange the evils in the Church for others greater. Often we are unwilling to tolerate a trivial evil and we provoke a greater one.' Like many others, Pirkheimer, who once had even joined the movement, wrote shortly before his death: 'We hoped that Romish knavery, the same as the rascality of the monks and priests, would be corrected; but, as is to be perceived, the matter has become worse to such a degree that the Evangelical knaves make the other knaves pious,' that is, the others still appear pious in comparison with the new unbridled preachers of liberty. But did not the father of the new movement himself acknowledge that 'our (people) are now seven times worse than they ever were before. We steal, lie, cheat, cram, and swill and commit all manner of vices.' 'We Germans are now the laughing-stock and the shame of all the countries, they hold us as shameful, nasty swine.' The same one that said this regrets to have been born a German, to have written and spoken German, and longs to fly from there, that he may not witness God's judgment breaking over Germany." (2)

"Merely with reference to the universal corruption among their own fellow believers, the very preachers and reformers of the Lutheran denomination had pronounced the judgment: 'We must in truth...confess: that, as every possible thing that means and can be called sin, vice, and shame has risen to its highest in Germany, it is much to be presumed that the evil spirits are nowhere else in the world save...in Germany alone.' 'The people would simply have to turn into devils; in human form there is no getting any worse.'" (2)

LUTHER HIMSELF ADMITS HE WAS NOT GUIDED BY GOD AND COULD BE WRONG

"Luther's advocates might, if their eyes are not filmed, read with profit the following words which their master penned when he had genuine misgivings at the outset of his apostasy. 'How many times,' he writes, 'have I not asked myself with bitterness the same question which the Papists put me: Art thou alone wise? Darest thou imagine that all mankind have been in error for so long a series of years? I am not so bold as to assert that I have been guided in this affair by God. How will it be, if, after all, it is thou thyself who art wrong, and art thou involving in error so many souls who will then be eternally damned?' (Latin Works, Weim. ed., 8, p. 411 seq.)." (O'Hare)

- - - - - - - - - - - - - - - -

CONCLUSION

Rather than engaging in 'celebrations' of 500 years of heresy (a Revolution or Deformation, NOT a Reformation!), and rather than lavishing praise on a lying heresiarch who destroyed families, emptied monasteries, laid waste to virtue, and waged unremitting war against Christ's Church (a vow-breaking apostate and true enemy of the Church who caused bloodshed, promoted sin, spread dangerous errors - doctrines approved by Satan! - and someone who has fostered the ruin of eternal souls), we should rightly be stepping up efforts at reparation & seeking ways to put an end to the damaging heresies of this 'Teacher of a Satanic Faith'. The lying teacher of the devil's doctrines should be rejected, not praised. To do otherwise, seems akin to aligning oneself with Judas, does it not? If such an enemy of truth is to be lauded by our prelates, we are indeed in a very sorry state. Keep in mind that any true doctrines that Luther may have taught, he learned from the very Church he so virulently hated and warred against. It is not to these that we have any objection. Yet we do not praise him for such either. Who praises any qualities of Lucifer since he fell? If the state of things today has Catholic bishops praising Luther, we may fear that praise for Lucifer may be next. God help us.

"I am amazed that you are so quickly forsaking the one who called you by (the) grace (of Christ) for a different gospel (not that there is another). But there

are some who are disturbing you and wish to pervert the gospel of Christ. But even if we or an angel from heaven should preach (to you) a gospel other than the one that we preached to you, let that one be accursed! As we have said before, and now I say again, if anyone preaches to you a gospel other than the one that you received, let that one be accursed! Am I now currying favor with human beings or God? Or am I seeking to please people? If I were still trying to please people, I would not be a slave of Christ." (St. Paul, Gal. 1:6-10)

- - - - - - - - - - - - - - - - -

Primary Sources:

(1) "Luther's Own Statements Concerning His Teaching and its Results. Taken Exclusively From the Earliest and Best Editions of Luther's German and Latin Works" by Henry O'Connor, S.J., 1885 A.D.

(2) "Luther and Lutherdom (From Original Sources)" [I] by Heinrich Denifle, O. P., 1904 A.D.

(3) "Exsurge Domine" (On Condemning The Errors Of Martin Luther), Pope Leo X, 1520 A.D.

(4) "A Catholic Dictionary" by Rev. W. E. Addis, 1887 A.D.

(5) "Decet Romanum Pontificem" (Papal Bull on the Excommunication of Martin Luther), Pope Leo X, 1521 A.D. (Online Source)

Note: Other sources may appear with passages.

- - - - - - - - - - - - - - - - -

"It is a certain, well-established fact that no other crime so seriously offends God and provokes His greatest wrath as the vice of heresy. Nothing contributes more to the ruin of provinces and kingdoms than this frightful pest." (St. Charles Borromeo)

PART 2:
SOME REFRESHERS

Contains Refreshers For These Topics...

**Sin | Hatred | Marriage
Divorce | Chastity
Adultery | Temperance
Priests | Pope | Prayer
Scripture Alone
Faith Alone
Deeds / Works**

MyCatholicSource.com Compilation:
Some Refreshers

Notice: Source information corresponding to numeric references in brackets below may be found after the conclusion in Part 1 above.

Some 'reality check' refreshers are provided herein which contrast Luther's corrupt behavior & teachings with Holy Scripture. Note that items contained within are not comprehensive. *[Reminder: Do not inflict (or wish) harm on yourself or others, break laws, take unsuitable / incautious or inappropriate / drastic actions, or take figurative items literally. We are not responsible for any interpretation / misinterpretation, application / misapplication, use / misuse, etc. of any item. Use of this material is subject to our terms of use.]*

- - -

Sin

Luther: "Be a sinner and sin boldly, but believe and rejoice in Christ even more boldly... No sin will separate us from [Christ], even though we commit fornication and murder a thousand times a day." (Letter from Luther to Philip Melanchthon, August 1, 1521 A.D.)

Reality Check: "If we sin deliberately after receiving knowledge of the truth, there no longer remains sacrifice for sins but a fearful prospect of judgment and a flaming fire that is going to consume the adversaries. Anyone who rejects the law of Moses is put to death without pity on the testimony of two or three witnesses. Do you not think that a much worse punishment is due the one who has contempt for the Son of God, considers unclean the covenant-blood by which he was consecrated, and insults the spirit of grace? We know the one who said: 'Vengeance is mine; I will repay,' and again: 'The Lord will judge his people.' It is a fearful thing to fall into the hands of the living God." (St. Paul, Heb. 10:26-31)

- - -

Hatred

Luther's Hatred: "The 'Reformer' and his followers were the very ones who conducted themselves as though the Divine Redeemer had positively commanded revenge and forbidden the love of one's enemy. To be convinced of this, one needs but read any book whatever by Luther, that hatred-filled and most biting of men." (2)

Reality Check: "You have heard that it was said, 'You shall love your neighbor and hate your enemy.' But I say to you, love your enemies, and pray for those who persecute you, that you may be children of your heavenly Father, for he makes his sun rise on the bad and the good, and causes rain to fall on the just and the unjust. For if you love those who love you, what recompense will you have? Do not the tax action does not damn him'; he only evidences his fall from faith." (2)

Reality Check: "Do you not know that the unjust will not inherit the kingdom of God? Do not be deceived; neither fornicators nor idolaters nor *adulterers* nor boy prostitutes nor practicing homosexuals nor thieves nor the greedy nor drunkards nor slanderers nor robbers will inherit the kingdom of God." (St. Paul, 1 Cor. 6:9-10, emphasis added)

- - -

Temperance

Luther: "As the apothecary was applying the tube [to Luther's dead body], he heard several loud winds discharged into the clyster-bag. In consequence of his intemperate eating and drink, Luther's body was wholly bloated with cachectic humors." (2)

Reality Check: "For the grace of God has appeared for the salvation of all men, and training us to reject godless ways and worldly desires and to live temperately, justly, and devoutly in this age, as we await the blessed hope, the appearance of the glory of the great God and of our savior Jesus Christ, who gave himself for us to deliver us from all lawlessness and to cleanse for himself a people as his own, eager to do what is good." (St. Paul, Ti. 2:11-14)

- - -

Priests

Luther: "U. Zasius had already said: 'I must first say that Luther with brazen shamelessness interprets the whole Scripture of the Old and New Testament, from the first book of the Bible to the end, against popes and priests, as if God, from the beginning of the world, had had no other business than to thunder against the priesthood.'" (2)

Reality Checks: "Honor God and respect the priest..." (Sirach 7:31) and "Whoever listens to you listens to me. Whoever rejects you rejects me. And whoever rejects me rejects the one who sent me." (Our Lord Jesus Christ, Lk. 10:16)

- - -

Pope

Luther: "Luther says: 'The Pope's Christ is the mother of the Devil.' That is to say, the Christ, in whom the Pope and the Catholics believe, is the mother of the Devil. Again: 'The Pope, the Cardinals, and the whole Romish Court and, mob, are nothing else but a stable full of big, coarse, stupid, disgraceful donkeys.'" (1)

Reality Check: "Jesus said to him in reply, 'Blessed are you, Simon son of Jonah. For flesh and blood has not revealed this to you, but my heavenly Father. And so I say to you, you are Peter, and upon this rock I will build my church, and the gates of the netherworld shall not prevail against it. I will give you the keys to the kingdom of heaven. Whatever you bind on earth shall be bound in heaven; and whatever you loose on earth shall be loosed in heaven." (Mt. 16:17-19)

- - -

Prayer

Luther: "On Sept. 9, 1521, [Luther] writes to Spalatin: 'Poor man that I am, I grow cold in spirit. I am still snoring on, and am lazy in prayer.'" (2)

Reality Checks: "Pray without ceasing" (St. Paul, 1 Thes. 5:17) and "The end of all things is at hand. Therefore, be serious and sober for prayers." (St. Peter, 1 Pt. 4:7)

- - -

Scripture Alone

Luther: "Scripture alone is the true lord and master of all writings and doctrine on earth." (Luther) [Online Sources]

Reality Check: "Therefore, brothers, stand firm and hold fast to the traditions that you were taught, either by an oral statement or by a letter of ours." (St. Paul, 2 Thes. 2:15)

- - -

Faith Alone

Luther: "Having rejected the authority of the Pope, he admits the authority of Satan; for he informs us in plain, unmistakeable words, that the Devil argued in favor of his doctrine of justification by faith alone..." (1)

Reality Check: "See how a person is justified by works and not by faith alone... For just as a body without a spirit is dead, so also faith without works is dead." (St. James, Jms. 2:24, 26)

- - -

Deeds / Works

Luther: "Luther's gospel with its fundamental thought, justification and forgiveness of sin by faith alone, led both theoretically and practically to the consequent proposition: therefore all the good works and everything we impose upon ourselves and do, are useless for salvation. Nay more, he who considers works as a necessary factor on the way of salvation exercises them 'without the blood of Christ,' consequently denies the Savior and Redeemer, puts his own work in the place of Christ, and is 'drowned' in a service of works." (2)

Reality Check: "I saw the dead, the great and the lowly, standing before the throne, and scrolls were opened. Then another scroll was opened, the book of life. The dead were judged according to their deeds, by what was written in the scrolls. The sea gave up its dead; then Death and Hades gave up their dead. All the dead were judged according to their deeds." (Rv. 20:12-13)

- - -

"Jesus Christ says: 'Hear the Church' (Mt. 18:17). 'No,' says Protestantism, 'do not hear the Church; protest against her with all your might.' Jesus Christ says: 'If any one will not hear the Church, look upon him as a heathen and a publican' (Mt. 18:17). 'No,' says Protestantism, 'if any one does not hear the Church, look upon him as an Apostle, as an ambassador of God.' Jesus Christ says: 'The gates of hell shall not prevail against my Church' (Mt. 16:18). 'No,' says Protestantism, 'it is false; the gates of hell have prevailed against the Church for a thousand years and more.' Jesus Christ has declared St. Peter, and every successor to St. Peter - the Pope - to be his Vicar on earth (Mt. 16:18, Jn. 21:15-17). 'No,' says Protestantism, 'the pope is the Antichrist.' Jesus Christ says: 'My yoke is sweet, and my burden is light' (Mt. 11:30). 'No,' said Luther and Calvin; 'it is impossible to keep the commandments.' Jesus Christ says: 'If thou wilt enter into life, keep the commandments.' (Mt. 19:17) 'No,' said Luther and Calvin, 'faith alone, without good works, is sufficient to enter life everlasting.' Jesus Christ says: 'Unless you do penance, you shall all likewise perish' (Lk. 13:3). 'No,' says Protestantism, 'fasting and other works of penance are not necessary in satisfaction for sin.' Jesus Christ says: 'This is my body' (Mt. 26:26, Mk. 14:22, Lk. 22:19, Jn. 6:55). 'No,' said Calvin, 'this is only the figure of Christ's body; it will become his body as soon as you receive it.' Jesus Christ says: 'I say to you, that whosoever shall put away his wife, and shall marry another, committeth adultery, and he that shall marry her that is put away, committeth

adultery' (Mt. 19:9). 'No,' says Protestantism to a married man, 'you may put away your wife, get a divorce, and marry another.' Jesus Christ says to every man: 'Thou shalt not steal' (Mt. 19:18). 'No,' said Luther to secular princes, 'I give you the right to appropriate to yourselves the property of the Roman Catholic Church.' The Holy Ghost says in Holy Scripture: 'Man knoweth not whether he be worthy of love or hatred' (Eccl. 9:1). 'Who can say, My heart is clean, I am pure from sin?' (Prov. 20:9); and, 'Work out your salvation with fear and trembling' (Philip. 2:12). 'No,' said Luther and Calvin, 'but whosoever believes in Jesus Christ is in the state of grace.' St. Paul says: 'If I should have faith, so that I could remove mountains, and have not charity, I am nothing' (1 Cor. 13:2). 'No,' said Luther and Calvin, 'faith alone is sufficient to save us.' St. Peter says that in the Epistles of St. Paul there are many things 'hard to be understood, which the unlearned and unstable wrest, as also the other Scriptures, to their own perdition' (2 Pt. 3:16). 'No,' says Protestantism, 'the Scriptures are very plain and easy to understand.' St. James says: 'Is any man sick among you? Let him bring in the priests of the Church, and let them pray over him, anointing him with oil, in the name of the Lord' (Jms. 5:14). 'No,' says Protestantism, 'that is a vain and useless ceremony.' Being thus impious enough to make liars of Jesus Christ, the Holy Ghost, and the Apostles, need we wonder if they continually slander Catholics, telling and believing worse absurdities about them than the heathens did?" (Muller)

PART 3:

IN CLOSING...

Contains...

Also Try / Additional Resources (Links)

Also Available...
**Apologetics App/Catholic Bible References
Catholic Bible Facts Book
Catholic Annual Prayer Book
700+ Consoling Thoughts From Holy Scripture**

**Did You Know?
Coming Soon
Have You Heard?**

Also Try / Additional Resources...

Reminder: Where applicable, <u>exclude extraneous hyphens which may appear in links below</u>. Any visit to our website(s) may require agreement to our terms. For more terms information, visit http://www.mycatholicsource.com/mcs/terms_of_use.htm.

Catholic Apologetics (Topic Page) - http://www.mycatholicsource.com/mcs/tp/topic_page-catholic_apologetics.htm

Biblical References For Various Catholic Beliefs - http://www.mycatholicsource.com/mcs/nc/non_catholics__biblical_references.htm

Non-Catholics Section [Incl. Challenges For Non-Catholics, Biblical References For Catholic Beliefs, Apologetics] - http://www.mycatholicsource.com/mcs/non-catholics.htm

Those Outside the Church (Topic Page) - http://www.mycatholicsource.com/mcs/tp/topic_page-those_outside_the_Church.htm

To Convert Is To Gain - http://www.mycatholicsource.com/mcs/nc/non_catholics__to_convert_is_to_gain.htm

Tips For Apologists - http://www.mycatholicsource.com/mcs/pc/coming_home/coming_home_tips.htm

Becoming a Catholic (Topic Page) - http://www.mycatholicsource.com/mcs/tp/topic_page-becoming_a_catholic.htm

Free Resources (Fliers that you may print & distribute) [Incl.: The Importance Of Being Catholic: Combating Religious Indifferentism; Non-Catholic 'Christians': Challenges (4-in-1 flier); Biblical References For Various Catholic Beliefs; Non-Catholic 'Christian' Challenge: Is Your Religion True?; Etc.] - http://www.mycatholicsource.com/mcs/resources/resources.htm

Coming Home Section - http://www.mycatholicsource.com/mcs/coming_home.htm

Coming Home Section Reflections - http://www.mycatholicsource.com/mcs/qt/coming_home_reflections.htm

Catholic Basics Section - http://www.mycatholicsource.com/mcs/catholic_basics.htm

Ten Commandments (Topic Page) - http://www.mycatholicsource.com/mcs/tp/topic_page-ten_commandments.htm

Sin (Topic Page) - http://www.mycatholicsource.com/mcs/tp/topic_page-sin.htm

Evil / Satan (Topic Page) -
http://www.mycatholicsource.com/mcs/tp/topic_page-evil_devil_satan.htm

Sacraments Section -
http://www.mycatholicsource.com/mcs/sacraments.htm

Priests (Topic Page) -
http://www.mycatholicsource.com/mcs/tp/topic_page-priest.htm

Pope (Topic Page) -
http://www.mycatholicsource.com/mcs/tp/topic_page-pope.htm

Vocations (Topic Page) -
http://www.mycatholicsource.com/mcs/tp/topic_page-vocations.htm

Why Priestly Celibacy? -
http://www.mycatholicsource.com/mcs/pc/vocations/why_priestly_celibacy.htm

Holy Matrimony (Topic Page) -
http://www.mycatholicsource.com/mcs/tp/topic_page-catholic_marriage.htm

Against Divorce (Topic Page) -
http://www.mycatholicsource.com/mcs/tp/topic_page-divorce.htm

Holy Sacrifice of the Mass (Topic Page) -
http://www.mycatholicsource.com/mcs/tp/topic_page-catholic_mass.htm

Holy Eucharist (Topic Page) -
http://www.mycatholicsource.com/mcs/tp/topic_page-Holy_Communion.htm

Jesus (Topic Page) -
http://www.mycatholicsource.com/mcs/tp/topic_page-Jesus.htm

Blessed Virgin Mary (Topic Page) -
http://www.mycatholicsource.com/mcs/tp/topic_page-Blessed_Virgin_Mary.htm

Saints (Topic Page) -
http://www.mycatholicsource.com/mcs/tp/topic_page-saints.htm

Holy Scripture (Topic Page) -
http://www.mycatholicsource.com/mcs/tp/topic_page-catholic_bibles.htm

Catholic Prayer (Topic Page) -
http://www.mycatholicsource.com/mcs/tp/topic_page-catholic_prayers.htm

Visit Here For Thousands Of Quotations From Popes, Saints, Scripture, Etc. Categorized By Section -
http://www.mycatholicsource.com/mcs/qt/reflections_categorized.htm

Looking For a Great Catholic Home Page? Try The MCS Daily Digest™ -
http://www.mycatholicsource.com/mcs/cg/mcs_daily_digest.asp

Looking For Something Else? Try Our Various Indexes For 15,000+ Entries -
http://www.mycatholicsource.com/mcs/help.htm

Also Available: Great Apologetics Resource - Catholic Bible References App

Place Hundreds Of Scripture References Concerning Catholic Beliefs At Your Fingertips!

Do you have a smart phone or tablet? Consider purchasing our 'Catholic Bible References' app. This "must have" apologetics tool presented by MyCatholicSource.com can be used to help Catholics discuss & defend the faith. It features hundreds of key Bible references conveniently arranged by topic, 100+ tips for locating related passages (including those useful for defending the Catholic faith among 'Jehovah's Witnesses' & Mormons), modern / traditional Scripture translations, easy / quick / comprehensive search, convenient index, selectable text (where available), Old Testament / New Testament indicator, a quick, easy-to-use interface, in-app e-mail, and in-app help.

Use To:

* Defend the Catholic Faith Using Scripture

* Be Prepared to Answer Biblical Questions About the Catholic Faith From Non-Catholics & Catholics Alike

* Educate Yourself in Biblical Truths of the Catholic Faith

* Refresh Your Memory

* Quickly Compare Translations

* Help Spread the Catholic Faith (Makes a Great Gift App!)

Topics Include: Ashes, Blessed Virgin Mary, Celibacy, Devil, Divinity of Christ, Faith / Works (Sola Fide/Faith Alone), Hell, Hierarchy, Incense, Indulgences, Infallibility, Intercession, Lord's Day / Sunday, Mass, Morality (Contraception, Fornication, Homosexuality, Etc.), Oral Tradition (Sola Scriptura/Bible Alone), Original Sin, Papacy, Prayer (Repeating Prayer, Praying for the Dead, Praying to Saints), Priest / Priesthood, Purgatory, Relics, Sacraments (Anointing of the Sick/Extreme Unction, Baptism, Confession, Confirmation, Eucharist, Holy Orders, Marriage), Saints, Salvation, Scripture, Trinity, Unity, And More...

Look for our 'Catholic Bible References' app where you buy apps!

For more information regarding our apps, please try here: http://www.mycatholicsource.com/mcs/cg/comrc/apps.htm

Notice: Features, system requirements, pricing, devices supported, availability, etc. are subject to change at any time without notice.

Thank You For Your Support!

Also Available: Catholic Bible Facts Book

Don't miss this handy 'information-filled' treasury of Catholic Bible facts!

Contains...

* More Than 250 'Bible Facts Q & A' (Questions Include: What does "Inspiration" of Holy Scripture refer to? What language was the Bible originally written in? What are deuterocanonical books? What is 'scriptural tropology'? What is the relation of the Old Testament to the New Testament? What is the Septuagint? Is Holy Scripture free from error? What are Scripture 'senses'? How many words are in the Bible? How should I choose a Bible? And more...)

* Coverage of Beatitudes, Parables, and Jesus' Emphasized Statements

* Bible Books (Info. & Lists), Psalms Lists

* More Than 50 Links For More Information

For more information, please try here: http://www.mycatholicsource.com/mcs/cg/comrc/media.htm

Please look for *'Catholic Bible Facts'* and other publications in our 'Catholic Educational Series' - as well as other MyCatholicSource.com publications / BFSMedia publications - where you purchased this title.

Thank You For Your Support!

Also Available: 'Catholic Annual Prayer Book'

Don't miss this daily prayer companion for Catholics that is 'suitable for any year'!

Let this tradition-minded MyCatholicSource.com compilation help boost your prayer life with many helpful resources, such as...

* 365+ Daily Prayers (Jan.-Dec.)

* Holiday/Seasonal Prayers (Advent/Christmas, Lent/Easter...)

* Daily Prayers (Morning, Evening/Bedtime, Daily Examination of Conscience...)

* Hundreds of Prayers Indexed by Title

* Nearly 200 Aspirations/Short Prayers

* Over 100 Latin Prayers & Aspirations

* 500+ Topics for Meditation

* Hundreds of Prayer Tips & Insights

* And More...

Includes prayers drawn from Holy Scripture, the liturgy, writings of popes & saints, the Raccolta, the Roman Breviary, the Roman Missal, etc.

For more information, please try here: http://www.mycatholicsource.com/mcs/cg/comrc/media.htm

Please look for *'Catholic Annual Prayer Book'* and other publications in our 'Catholic Devotional Series' - as well as other MyCatholicSource.com publications / BFSMedia publications - where you purchased this title.

+ + +

"Prayer is man's richest boon. It is his light, his nourishment, and his very life, for it brings him into communication with God, who is light, nourishment, and life." (Dom Gueranger)

+ + +

Thank You For Your Support!

Also Available: 700+ Consoling Thoughts From Holy Scripture

Biblical Consolation, Comforting Words, Positive Thoughts & Encouragement For Catholics In Times of Sadness, Sorrow, Grief, Illness, Trial, Persecution, Or Any Time

A #1 New Release on Amazon.com! (Kindle Version, 5/18)

+ + +

"Some of the most consoling & comforting words from Holy Scripture, all in one place!"

The Bible tells the greatest TRUE love story ever told and - along with imparting to us much knowledge & instruction - it can also bring great comfort. But the Bible is a very long work and there may be times when Catholics simply want to quickly reflect on some consoling, comforting, positive, or encouraging words from Scripture. On such occasions, we hope you will find this publication to be a wonderful aid.

This book may be particularly useful for...

* Providing consolation & comfort

* Strengthening & encouraging

* Providing a scriptural 'pick-me-up' / uplift

* Increasing hope

* Helping persons feel & trust that God loves and cares for them

* Increasing one's love of God - the greatest & first commandment (see Mt. 22:37-38)

Great for...

* Devotional reading

* Daily meditation

* Times of sadness, sorrow, grief, illness, trial or persecution - or any time

Designed for faithful Catholics, this publication includes...

* More than 700 selections, drawn from both the Old & New Testaments

* Dozens of scripture related reflections from popes & saints

* Links for additional resources

* List of Books of the Bible

You may be glad to know, this publication utilizes a traditional (English language) Catholic Scripture translation (Douay-Rheims), which is based on the Latin Vulgate Bible. The Vulgate is the only formally 'canonized' translation of Holy Scripture.

We hope you will find this pleasant & uplifting publication - which is 'filled with biblical comfort for faithful Catholics' - to be both encouraging & inspiring.

+ + +

Get your copy today! Also makes a great gift!

+ + +

"The Holy Scripture or Bible is the collection of sacred, inspired writings through which God has made known to us many revealed truths. Some call them letters from Heaven to earth, that is, from God to man." (Baltimore Catechism)

"Learn the Heart of God in the words of God, that you may long more ardently for things eternal." (Pope St. Gregory the Great, Doctor of the Church)

+ + +

For more information, please try here:
http://www.mycatholicsource.com/mcs/cg/comrc/media.htm

Please look for *'700+ Consoling Thoughts From Holy Scripture'* and other publications in our 'Catholic Devotional Series' - as well as other MyCatholicSource.com publications / BFSMedia publications - where you purchased this title.

Thank You For Your Support!

Did You Know?

Content from this publication may also appear in our 'Catholics And Ecumenism' book. This book also contains special bonuses such as 'Is The Catholic Church The Only True Church?', 'The Importance Of Being Catholic', and more...

For more information, please try here: http://www.mycatholicsource.com/mcs/cg/comrc/media.htm

Please look for *'Catholics And Ecumenism: Why Do Traditionalists Disapprove Of False Ecumenism? Doesn't This Go Against 'The Council' (Vatican II)?'* and other publications in our 'Catholic Controversy Series' - as well as other MyCatholicSource.com publications / BFSMedia publications - where you purchased this title.

Thank You For Your Support!

Coming Soon

Please look for upcoming apologetics publications - as well as other future MyCatholicSource.com publications / BFSMedia publications - where you purchased this title.

Note: For additional information concerning our books, please try here: http://www.mycatholicsource.com/mcs/cg/comrc/media.htm

Thank You For Your Support!

Have You Heard?

Ratings *really* matter!

If you enjoyed this book, please consider leaving a positive review. Note that 5-star reviews may be very helpful in spreading the word.

Thank You & God Bless You!

+ + +

"Graciously hear the prayers of Thy Church, we beseech Thee, O Lord; that her enemies and all heresies may be brought to naught, and that she may serve Thee in perfect security and freedom. Through Christ our Lord. Amen." (Roman Missal)

+ + +